The Buddha Made Me Do It

A memoir by
Marla Martenson

D1590623

Author's Note:

This is a true story and the characters are real, as are the events. However some names, descriptions, and locations have been changed for privacy reasons. Some characters, and situations have been condensed and the chronology adjusted for narrative purposes. Otherwise, this story represents the truth of my experiences.

©2016 Marla Martenson

ISBN-10: 0-9975664-0-X
ISBN-13: 978-0-9975664-0-6

Cupid's Press
Los Angeles, CA

Also by Marla Martenson
Diary of a Beverly Hills Matchmaker
Hearts On The Line
Amateur Night

Acknowledgments

I am truly thankful to the following people for their various roles in my life and journey, which include their assistance, guidance, encouragement, support, inspiration, friendship and insight, beginning with my editor extraordinaire, friend, and mentor, Peggy Lang; Robbie Adkins for the beautiful book cover; and Julie McCarron for going on this amazing journey with me. Jenn Oliver (Sidekick Jenn) for her wonderful formatting and Laird Sapir for her beautiful work on my website.

For being a catalyst in my transformation, I am grateful to Goddess Tauheedah and the whole wonderful gang at The Imagine Center; to my Reiki Master Katt Lowe; Grace Cavanaugh and Osairah; Herbal Thom; Karen A. Dahlman; Linda Salvin; Tina Louise Spalding; Joanna DeVoe; Jimmy Mack; Mimi Donaldson; Linda Deir and her wonderful husband Ray; Dr. Moe; Steffany Barton, (Go Angels!); the uncommon urban shaman Harry Paul; the Candle Magick Mavin Vicky Adams; Paul Selig; Master healer/shaman Deborah King and The Spiritual Catalyst Teal Swan.

Where would I be without the support of Rouben Terzian, Bob Guccione Jr., My Tigress Sister Snezana Adamovic, August McLaughlin, Kyra Davis, Victoria Moran, Rockin' Robin Abb, George Noory, Megan Castran, Mark Miller, and the awesome residents of Kloshe Illahee.

I am so blessed and grateful to my heavenly team; my guardian angels, Murth, Thomas, and all of my spirit guides; my loving father and brother who are on the other side; Larry and Brett Martenson; and my dear friend Fran Marion—may you raise hell up there beyond the pearlies, keeping the party going. I must also offer a unique thank-you to Edgar Allan Poe.

For Macie Martenson's constant devotion, companionship, and wagging tail, I am humbly grateful. And Romeo the Chihuahua, you too made a difference.

Special thanks to my whole matchmaking team who are the reason I'm not standing on the corner with a tin cup.

And much love and gratitude for my adoring husband Adolfo, and my mother Donna Reed for their love and support.

Blessings, love, peace, joy and angel kisses transmitting from my heart to yours on this exciting journey called life!

Marla

xoxo

What Others Are Saying About This Book

"This is the ultimate girls' guide to the spiritual life: fresh and funny and down to earth, even when Martenson has us contemplating the mysteries of existence. If you've ever wished for a soul sister on your path to enlightenment, she's here for you. And she's fun."
— Victoria Moran, author of a *Creating a Charmed Life* and *The Good Karma Diet*

"Marla Martenson's unchained optimism shines through every word of this spiritual memoir. She is a woman who leans into life with charming levity and a writer who delights in wrapping her discoveries in laughter. Join her in this quest to uncover life's magick and perhaps tap into some of your own!"
— Joanna DeVoe, author of *The Rich Witch*

"Join Marla on her entertaining road to enlightenment through divine intervention, wacky adventures and belly laughs that includes a lively and eventful cast of characters. It's a lesson in spiritual hopscotch where Marla's desire to fully jump in and participate with the otherworldly dimensions and energies magically evokes the fun!"
— Karen A. Dahlman, Psychotherapist and author of *The Spirit of Alchemy: Secret Teachings of the Sacred Reunion*

"Marla Martenson writes a highly engaging story about exploring the mystical while firmly tethered to the tangible and complicated material challenges of the modern world. Both funny and sweet, it's a book that will entertain spiritualists and skeptics alike."

— Kyra Davis, New York Times bestselling author of *Just One Night*

"A delicious blend of wit and spirituality, The Buddha Made Me Do It will make you laugh out loud while digging deeper into your own sacred journey."

— August McLaughlin, author of *Embraceable*

"Often, the funniest thing about the multitude of spiritual offerings in Los Angeles is the complete lack of humor with which they're presented. Marla Martenson remedies this in her new memoir, The Buddha Made Me Do It, which adds generous helpings of humorous insight to the quest for spirituality. You'll never look at yoga, meditation, and crystal healing with a straight face again."

— Mark Miller, author of *500 Dates: Dispatches From the Front Lines of the Online Dating Wars*

Content

The Buddha Caper

"I sense an intelligence rendered clairvoyant by feeling. I sense an artist." ~ Anaïs Nin

I wasn't exactly lost that day in early October, but when Buddha kind of accidentally (or maybe on purpose) helped me get somewhere, my life opened up like a dusty box of priceless jewelry.

I was purging clutter like a maniac when my Buddha adventure began. Maybe I didn't quite know what I wanted and needed, but I could definitely get rid of what I didn't need, the SICLW (Shit I Can Live Without). Each time a certain antsy clearing energy possessed me, I think I was trying to make room for something new to enter my life, though I told myself I was just honoring a vow that my husband Adolfo and I made not to turn into one of those couples who can no longer park the car in the garage. Routinely shedding SICLW, I often scanned the cupboards, closets, nooks, and crannies for items to donate.

I tossed knick-knacks, some worn out gym clothes, motivational cassette tapes from the 80's, and a few books I never planned to read again. *Eject, toss, bag* was my mantra that day. Like the sacred snakes of ancient Crete considered to be a symbol of rebirth, I was shedding old skin. I had no idea I was about to coil the arm of the goddess.

A wooden Buddha statuette took up room on a shelf, the gift of a former neighbor. Did I need him? We had since moved from Hollywood, out of a cramped, carpeted, cottage-cheese-ceilinged, paper-thin-walled apartment with temperamental plumbing, to our very own dream home with three bedrooms, a formal dining room, two-car garage and a pool, fifteen miles north in the San Fernando Valley.

Now, I will admit that on *occasion* I have taken the liberty of donating some of Adolfo's SHCLW-IMHO (Shit *He* Can Live Without, In My Humble Opinion.) In this case, though, I promise you that Buddha was my shit! Not that I didn't like the Buddha, mind you. Even now, I wonder why I felt the need to donate the little statue, but in the three years that we lived in the new house, not even once did Adolfo ever think about the Buddha or ask about the statue. Without another thought, I did the deed. I placed Buddha in the bag with the other SICLW and dropped him off at his new home, the Goodwill.

THE VERY NEXT DAY, Adolfo inquired, "Hey, honey, what ever happened to that wooden Buddha? Have you seen it?"

Kee-rap!

Pause to explain my very own bylaw to the honesty in marriage code: if hubby has control-freak storm episodes that are intense and awful yet tend to blow over and be totally forgotten and is otherwise adoring and adorable, it's not only okay but vitally essential to the continuance of the union if wifey finds it necessary to exaggerate, vacillate, equivocate, obfuscate, and, okay, prevaricate occasionally at her discretion. The same bylaw does not apply to him. Fair enough, right?

"Nope, mi amor," I said, "I haven't seen it. Must still be packed away somewhere in boxes from the move."

"You didn't get rid of it, did you, Marlita?"

"Whaaaat?" The man is on some dang wavelength with me. "Nooooo-hooo! Of course not! Why would I do that? But hey, if I did, what's the diff? It's MY Buddha..."

"It's *OUR* Buddha. Marlita, are you saying you got rid of it? Because you had better not have gotten rid of it. That's just typical! You get rid of things before even asking me!"

"Adolfo, I did not get rid of it, of course not. I would never do that. I will look for it, don't worry. Be right back."

Instead of searching, I stepped into the bathroom. *Breathe, Marlita, breathe.*

I checked several times in the ensuing week at the Goodwill for the damn Buddha. No Buddhas of any kind. Not one. Adolfo checked on a daily basis whether I'd found it yet, and I couldn't equivocate, obfuscate, or prevaricate any longer. It was time to innovate.

I'd seen little Buddhas in spiritual bookshops and yoga studios all over Los Angeles. I would just go buy another one. Adolfo would never know the difference. I hustled over to Hollywood and checked out at least half a dozen spiritual hot spots with no luck whatsoever. How could that be?

Back over the hill to the valley, I popped into three places that I knew of. Nothing. I Googled more stores and found a listing in Tarzana. Driving down Ventura Boulevard, I decided that this would be my last stop. If this place didn't have any wooden Buddhas, I would give up and face the consequences. I do realize this makes me sound like

Lucy Ricardo, a character whose situational pickles greatly enhanced the world's ability to laugh at itself. As a redhead married to a Latin musician, I feel a close bond. I definitely love Lucy.

Bells jingled as I opened the door to The Imagine Center. A peaceful ambience and calming energy filled the small space, packed with lovely crystals, books, jewelry, and all sorts of things someone on a spiritual path would need in her bag of tricks. What I did not see were any Buddha statues, wooden or otherwise. I chatted with the lovely woman at the cash register, and she confirmed that they did not carry what I was looking for, but she handed me a flyer and encouraged me to come back anytime.

The flyer announced that The Imagine Center held classes, each only fifteen dollars. A six-week course starting on Thursday night would teach me to create abundance. Since the book club that my friend Julie and I had belonged to recently disbanded due to scheduling difficulties and babysitters—Julie and I were the only childless members—I was looking for something stimulating that would also get me out of the house more often. This class sounded like a possibility. As I left the shop, a memory came to me. My parents had one of those foot high golden Buddha statues in the living room that were popular in the 60's. And we also had a wooden Buddha cookie jar, which my mother still has. When I was a baby, my mother used to point at the statue and the cookie jar and repeat, "Buddha, Buddha." My first word wasn't mama or dada it was Buddha!

I started the engine of my red Toyota and inserted the pods of my hands-free headset into my ears. "SIRI!" I commanded, "call Julie!"

SIRI performed and Julie answered as I pulled out of the parking lot. "Hey, girlie, what's up?"

"I've driven all over Los Angeles in search of that damn Buddha. All I can do now is pray that Adolfo forgets about it."

"Oh, Marla, you know he will." Julie's wise-woman, occasionally wise-ass, voice comforted me instantly. "He'll be onto something else in a few days. With his OCD tendencies, just wait, he'll be harping on which way the forks are facing in the kitchen drawer!"

"You are so right! I'm sticking to my story, adding that the Buddha must have gotten lost in the move." Then, mood shifting to optimism, I told her about the cool spiritual gift shop and the classes on abundance.

Either that, she said, or we could start a new book group for dog-moms only, reading the best dog-related books available. "So, canines...or abundance?"

It was dark already at 5:00 PM when I drove the three-minute trip to Julie's house. I had to wait while she finished a last-minute email to Jason Priestly, for whom she was ghost-writing his memoir. On Julie's BarcaLounger—I'm not making that up—her alert two-pound Chihuahua, Romeo, snarled at me, perhaps sensing his mistress had chosen an abundance class over dog adulation because of me. I may have been taking his growls a bit too personally, but after two years, I had yet to be deemed worthy of even approaching his energy field, let alone petting him.

Julie appeared from the bedroom wearing an emerald green top, jeans, and green ballet slippers studded with bling.

"Nice outfit, perfect for attracting abundance!"

"Thanks, I need all the help I can get right now in that department! How was your day?"

I told her about a couple I matched up last year who just got engaged. "And I signed up a new client, and, oh... I taught Macie how to jump through a Hula Hoop. That makes thirteen tricks so far!"

Romeo shot me a dirty look and turned his back to me.

A full October moon shone auspiciously as we drove to Tarzana. We entered a tiny, dimly lit, yet mystical-feeling, room in the back of the shop. Candlelight flickered off of the colorful crystals as we breathed in the smell of incense. Eight women sat on folding chairs, and Julie and I took seats toward the front, notebooks open and pens poised, ready to learn how to attract a cascade of abundance in our lives.

A statuesque African American woman with long corn-rows, elegant features, and a commanding presence took a seat facing the class. She introduced herself as Goddess Tauheedah, our teacher and the owner of The Imagine Center. In the soft lighting, I couldn't tell if Julie's expression meant what-the-hell-did-you-get-me-into or not. After much discussion and inquiries from students on whether Goddess Tauheedah was her real name, and whether we should call her Goddess or Tauheedah, the class began. Tauheedah assured us of the goddess within us all.

She explained that abundance is our birthright, and that we must trust in the Universal channel of abundance. She also explained that everyone should have an altar in their home, preferably in the Southwest corner of the room.

"When working at the altar, call in the angels of abundance. They will come!"

I felt wonderful. I loved being there with like-minded people, soaking up the good vibes and learning new techniques to create some magic in our lives. I was and still am mesmerized by Tauheedah's knowledge, confidence, and her certainty of connection to the divine. I want to be like her. I see her as the kind of artist Anaïs Nin described.

That very first class stirred my whole being. If that sounds trite, it's because we just don't have spiritual vocabularies that can transcend the two-dimensional page. We need words that leap through time like cosmic grasshoppers, zipping backwards and forwards, or plunging like Pisces fish, reflected in the darkest depths, yet heightening the now. I thought of Buddha, gaining enlightenment after a night under the Bodhi tree, the blue lotus blooming nearby. It was what he brought to that night, though, that opened the moonlit portal. What I brought to Tauheedah's class allowed me to stand near a portal, close enough to see the stars.

I had read my first book on the Law of Attraction when I was twenty-seven years old. A co-worker told me about this little red book that was written in 1925 by a woman named Florence Scovil Shinn. I still have that book today and have reread it many times over, as well as her other books, *The Secret Door To Success*, *Your Word Is Your Wand*, and *The Power Of The Spoken Word*.

The first line in her *Game of Life* reads:

Most people consider life a battle, but it is not a battle, it is a game. It is a game, however which cannot be played successfully without the knowledge of spiritual law.

Those laws require devotion. Florence Scovil Shinn was a great believer in the use of affirmations. She lists many affirmations in all of her books. I quickly adopted the use of affirmations, some of them from her books, and two of which I still repeat on a daily basis.

God is my unfailing supply, and large sums of money come to me quickly, under grace, in perfect ways.

I have a magical work in a magical way; I give magical service for magical pay.

That little red book opened my mind and stirred in my heart what I already knew to be true deep in my soul. At the time, I was married (an unfortunate decision fueled by hormones) to my former husband, a gorgeous and talented French chef. Working as a waitress—a job that exhausted me and depleted my soul—and scrambling with all of the other dreamers in Hollywood, running to auditions, hoping to get that big acting break. Even though my life didn't exactly line up in order and flow the way I wanted it to, I did possess something special. I was born with an unchained optimism, seeing the bright side of things, knowing that everything would be all right. I always sense that something incredible is on the verge of happening.

As the years passed, I continued my spiritual practice by going to lectures, reading books, listening to tapes and putting the Law of Attraction in use on a regular basis with my prayers, affirmations, and vision boards. I magically created a life that I had only dreamed of, which included finally leaving the restaurant business behind, and starting my own business, owning a house, and becoming a published author. No one is more surprised than I am that I am a successful, well-known, high-end matchmaker for affluent men, hob-knobbing with millionaires and billionaires as I help them to find love.

From the outside, my career looks easy, fun, rewarding and full of excitement. Usually, it is, and I am incredibly grateful to be my own boss, work from home, make my own schedule, and earn a good living. No one is pulling my strings, and that is just the way I like it. Sometimes I feel like I should pinch myself to affirm I'm not in a dream, but then, of course, life does that little service for me.

I also felt the presence of a weighted chain that night, tethering me to harsh issues. Every time a client turns down a match I've worked hard to line up, or threatens a lawsuit because the women he has met haven't been "hot enough," "young enough," "thin enough," or "busty enough," tiny daggers pierce my soul, and my ego whispers odious suggestions in my ear... Marla, tell these bastards off! They are sick in the mind, have jaded sensibilities; they are shallow, only concerned with the part of their anatomy that readily fluctuates in size! I want to say to them, how can you reach this age and not know that young flesh, a visage without lines is fleeting? You idiots, I want to yell, stop demanding inflated breasts with nipples the size of a quarter—not a nickel or a poker chip, as some actually have the nerve to specify—whereupon I make it clear that I don't provide such a service, nearly frothing over with suppressed frustration. Mature men with bald pates and pot bellies imagine themselves as Dorian Grays, forever young and handsome, and worthy of the most exquisite young women in the Universe to share their lives with. We all have our dreams, and that is theirs, but deep down I know theirs is self-defeating. I want to tell them they need to go deep, into the blue, into the light, soul to soul to begin to scratch the itch they are feeling.

With each of their appraisals, I am obligated to superficially rate each woman that applies for my service, reducing her value on a limited scale of one to ten, assessing whether her looks qualify her as worthy of my clients' standards. I see the inner goddesses in some of these women, but rate her outer package like she is a USDA cut of meat. This damages me.

I sit at my altar, in prayer, communing with angels, seeking peace, enlightenment, a peek beyond the veil, yet I'm living a double life. There is a disconnect when, after my meditation, I sit down at my desk to search for anorexic women with huge tits to please shallow fuckwits. Sometimes I know just how Lorena Bobbitt felt, and that truly scares me. My alternating universes are giving me spiritual whiplash. Can I continue to straddle both worlds and remain a free woman? I needed to know.

So, that was where I was that night with Julie in Goddess Tauheedah's class, not really imagining the world that would open up. Note to self: buy a garden Buddha to thank him for leading me along the path of enlightenment. Care to join me? I'll shine a light and hold the portal open for you. Come on in, my goddess sister!

The Bamboo Beating

"Religion is for people who are scared to go to hell. Spirituality is for people who have already been there." ~ Bonnie Raitt

I confess I was nervous as I prepared to face the music man—Adolfo. Once he saw what I'd done, his anger would be stupefying.

I'd come so far, and so my stomach shouldn't have been in a knot. My throat shouldn't have felt like I was choking back my feelings.

Since my first class with Goddess Tauheedah, I'd made some simple changes in my life and taken more classes at the Imagine Center as well. Julie and I had attended some fascinating spiritual workshops there and could discuss esoteric ideas like the Akashic records, chakras, auras, and channeling as easily as we chattered about massages and mani-pedis. I was still learning about this fusion of ancient-yet-evolving ways of looking at the mysteries of life.

I'd also returned to meditating on a regular basis, not every day, but at least a few times per week for these past three months of classes. For a Gemini hummingbird mind like mine that flits around in constant need of the nectar of mental stimulation, this was, in itself, miraculous. I was also becoming more aware of fears and emotional overloads that block my chakras. I learned that any issue, whether health-related or emotional, creates a corresponding hormonal response. The upside is that we can learn to allow that process to work for us. The downside is that it can block or reroute the earth-life-universe exchange of energy. I was pretty much in the downside that evening.

So, I entered my serene "zen" space that I'd cleared with dried sage and Palo Santo. I took deep, cleansing breaths and said my prayers and affirmations, kneeling beside my new altar with its collection of beautiful and powerful crystals, the Tibetan singing bowl, the miniature statues of Jesus, Mary, and a few saints, and different colored candles for manifesting and other rituals.

I was feeling centered after a twenty minute meditation. Pretty much.

And yet, heat rose through my body like hellfire. My meditation had apparently summoned my *kundalini* energy to...oh, hell. I was just scared.

What could I tell Adolfo? I had gotten a little carried away in my spiritual quest. Adolfo was about to find out, and when he did, well, I couldn't even manage to come up with a visualization of a positive outcome.

When Julie and I started this fascinating journey, we approached it as something to do together, girlfriends bonding over a new hobby. It was our little secret society of sorts, summoning the magic and mysteries that lay dormant deep within us. Recently, however, Julie casually mentioned a four-week workshop on Candle Magick that she had been taking at The Green Man Store. My ego tiptoed out and tugged on my ear. *Julie is taking a class without us?*

I had never heard of this Green Man Store. It sounded intriguing, but why hadn't she asked me if I wanted to take this class? I love candles. I wanted to learn how to dress candles for manifesting too. I hadn't even thought of signing up for a class without Julie. But then again, why not? Why couldn't we each advance on our own path, together *and* separately? I chastised myself. *Marla, you silly soul, what were you thinking?* Busy with my work, I let the Candle Magick issue drop.

But then I couldn't stop myself from thinking, what if she was getting more advanced than I was in her powers of manifestation? Again, I wavered, chiding myself. I was much too enlightened to suffer pangs of jealousy over a candle class.

Still...I supposed it wouldn't hurt to step it up a notch if enlightenment was what I was truly pursuing. The Buddha found enlightenment under a tree, but that was only after searching for it for decades. The great yogis and gurus did drastic things like subsist on five almonds a day in mountain caves for years. If I roamed the wilderness, nearly starved, and hallucinated for forty days, everyone would think I was nuts, but, of course, billions worship Jesus, a man who did just that.

So, in order to progress, I needed something powerful, something that neither Julie, nor anyone else that I knew for that matter, would ever do.

And I found it, all right, something nobody in their right mind would do. And it left mementos all over my body. Which Adolfo would soon see.

I rose up from my altar and padded across the hardwood floor in my bare feet to the bathroom to take a shower before going to bed. Adolfo was at work and wouldn't be home until after midnight. Standing in my underwear, I examined myself in the full-length mirror and cringed. It would take at least a week for the bruises to fade. As if my skin were an impressionist palette, its coloring shifted from red to purple, blue, and yellow up and down my hips and legs. My back was also covered in red circles, and a vampire-esque bite mark crusted with dried blood graced my upper right butt cheek. My body hurt, yes, but somehow I felt a tinge of that good kind of hurt. Imagine how, after running a twenty-eight mile marathon, the body aches with satisfaction that something has been accomplished. That line of reasoning wouldn't cut it with Adolfo.

How in the hell could I conceal this from him? My passionate Latin husband would undoubtedly want to be intimate soon. And even if a miraculously potent sun flare were to somehow cause his libido to wane for a week, my hot flashes and night sweats alone would have me peeling off my PJ's in no time.

So, here's how my skin became an art project: I paid someone to beat me with bamboo. Beat. Yes, with bamboo. Ha! Top that Julie, darling!

So how did a smart goddess like me get involved with something so drastic?

A week earlier I happened to be up in Thousand Oaks to meet with a client. Afterwards I stopped at one of my favorite places called The Healing Tree. They have soothing teas, healing herbs, medicinal tonics, and my new favorite beverage, homemade *kombucha*. The owner, Moe, a boyishly good-looking young doctor of Chinese medicine, conducted various healing modalities in the back room, and I had heard wonderful testimonials about his curative powers. Up until that day, I had not met Dr. Moe, who had invented a procedure he called Percussion Therapy. Many of the clients claimed that it was "life-changing."

Well, that day, Dr. Moe himself was there, just finishing up assisting a young woman select some tea to help with her insomnia. After he handed the woman her fifteen-dollar bag of tea, I introduced myself.

"I absolutely love your place," I gushed, "and your *kombucha* is to die for!"

He carefully looked me up and down. "I read auras," he stated, matter-of-factly. "You have some stagnation of energy around your right leg."

"*Really?*" My right leg *had* been bothering me lately, especially at night. An excruciating pain shot up and down, disturbing my sleep. How could he know this? I decided to trust him and explained my symptoms.

"Yes, well, I can see that. The right side is the male side."

"The male side?" That sort of made sense. Adolfo and I had been going through a particularly arduous time. He didn't take too well to my exuberant interest in the mystical. Besides the cost of the workshops, lectures, crystals, card readings, aura cleansings, and magical doodads, Adolfo was not pleased with my ideas on channeling, angels, fairies, extraterrestrials, astral travel, and orbs. I have an extremely open mind. Who am I to say that these things don't exist? Until someone can prove otherwise, I am fascinated in exploring the possibilities. Delving into the metaphysical side of things makes life sparkle. But Adolfo had one word to sum it all up: "fantasyland." According to him, I was "out of reality."

He had shared his unsolicited opinions with me in the form of a rant. "Marlita, come on!" he said. "Angels don't exist. They're a fantasy that people made up. And whatever you do, please, do NOT talk about it in front of my friends or family. I really think you might be going crazy. I mean, if you were standing in front of a judge, and you told him the things you are doing, he would immediately send you to the loony bin!"

Adolfo's strong reaction to my newfound interests hurt deeply, his words pummeling me like a fist in the gut. Debating the issue has never changed his mind. Neither did pleading with him to let me have my views without a running commentary from him. One approach that had a spiritual justification was not to engage. I would thank him for sharing and leave the room. That sometimes worked. I think about the "witches" of Salem who were burned at the stake for what I was now free to participate in, which was nothing more than honing my intuition, communing with the divine, and marveling at the unknown wonders of the Universe. I was hurting no one. My spiritual sisters did not have the luxury back then that I do. I carry their struggle in my soul.

Adolfo's criticism only hardened my resolve to delve deeper into my studies. I was determined to prove him wrong in the end—not really as a goal or some egoistic need to be right. I just had this one fantasy that someday, all would be revealed, and Adolfo would turn to me and say, "Holy crap! Marlita, you were right all along, I am so sorry that I doubted you! UFOs *are* real, and I can feel my guardian angel by my side." Okay, he doesn't have to go quite that far, but I'd love for him to have a meaningful spiritual experience we could share.

But until that day, I had to find a way to live with the opposition.

Or not.

I had a deep love for this man, and I knew that he adored me and would literally take a bullet for me. He'd expressed this to me many times. His devotion was unquestionable, but at what point must I save myself? If he only loved his concept of who I should be and how I should act and what I should say and to whom—was that really love of *me*?

Many a night I have gazed into the stars—at least the few that are visible in the San Fernando Valley—and focused on Orion, the constellation that the pyramids were aligned by. We are ancient beings, souls on a never ending journey through the cosmos, gliding in and out of lifetimes, learning lessons, working out the kinks, the karma, and hopefully evolving to our utmost potential. This process is ever more compelling and sacred to me. I could not be with someone who locked the gate. I had to go out and discover and experiment.

So.

"Dr. Moe, what can I do?" I asked the handsome young Chinese "doctor" that Thursday afternoon. "How can I unstagnate my energy? Do you think that your percussion therapy would be helpful?"

With a nod, Dr. Moe confidently affirmed that it would. I immediately booked an appointment; after all, $105.00 to get on the road to unclogging my aura and even possibly changing my life? What a bargain!

I'd arrived promptly at noon and chatted briefly with Jason, a *verrry* cute twenty-something yoga teacher and a regular at The Healing Tree. He was sitting with a couple of friends sipping tea and munching some freeze-dried mushrooms and sweet plums. Jason said he'd had percussion therapy a couple of months ago, and it was incredible and yes, life-changing. I wished I had more time to chat with him and find out what his exact experience was and how it changed him, but Dr. Moe was ready for me.

"Wish me luck," I chirped excitedly over my shoulder as I was escorted into a small room with two comfy chairs. As we sipped hot tea, we chatted about my energy levels, sleep patterns, and more. After taking a quick look at my tongue and taking my pulse, he then led me into an even smaller room that had a massage table in the middle. There were shelves and a glass cabinet against one wall, which housed a dozen or so cups. I knew immediately that they were for something called cupping therapy. I had read about the therapy, but had yet to try it. The application of suction cups of various sizes on the body, allows for the fascia (connective tissue of the body) to separate from the skin and muscles in order to unblock stagnation of Qi, (energy) thereby promoting healthy circulation. By focusing on superficial and middle layers of tissue, the process is intended to detoxify the whole body and various organs as well as clearing the emotions.

Cupping therapy dates back to ancient Egyptian, Chinese, and Middle Eastern cultures. One of the oldest medical textbooks in the world, the *Ebers Papyrus*, describes how the ancient Egyptians were using cupping therapy in 1,550 B.C. Cupping therapy is incredibly popular in China. I recently saw a video online of people getting it done on street corners. So, the process has certainly withstood the test of time.

Another shelf housed a large glass container filled with water and what I was pretty sure were leeches. The dark slimy creatures looked like stubby slithery worms swimming around. They disgusted me, and I quickly focused my attention on undressing down to my underwear and T-shirt.

Lying on one side, I felt Dr. Moe "scrape" my upper right leg quite forcefully.

"Before I utilize the bamboo sticks, I use this wooden tool to scrape the skin, which allows the stagnant Qi to move. This detoxifies the body, emotions, and various organs, and focuses on the superficial layers of the skin and tissue," he explained.

The scraping alone felt like it would bruise me. I was relieved when it was over, but then he picked up the two bamboo sticks.

Dr. Moe commenced to play my leg as if he were Buddy Rich, and the tympanic section of my body stretched all the way from a couple of inches above my right ankle up to the hip. He jammed on my upper leg, which sounded like fleshy tomatoes splatting against a wall.

The tapping or beating, was not done with much force, but the pain astonished me. I have never felt such excruciating agony in my life—with the possible exception of a certain bikini wax job a few years back. With every tap, my skin burned as if it had caught fire. I took deep breaths, moaned, whimpered, and then let out a few screams, followed by coyote-like yelps. I wondered what Jason and the patrons on the other side of the door sipping tea must think.

"Dr. Moe," I asked through clenched teeth, "what exactly is this doing?"

He gave me a variation of the same answer. "Allowing trauma, emotions, and inflammation to be expressed out of the body to allow for circulation. This detoxifies the body, emotions, and various organs, and focuses on the deepest layer of muscular tissue."

SHIT! GODDAMN! MOTHERFUCKER, THAT HURTS!
Sorry, but my thoughts had abruptly turned non-spiritual.

I gasped, "Oh...really? Hot damn, this hurts, Moe." Teeth still gritted. "Do your other clients scream too?"

"Hahaha, sometimes they do," he admitted. "I had one guy let out a primal guttural howl like a wild animal! It was crazy!"

That didn't seem at all crazy to me.

Dr. Moe continued the assault. "Oooh... here it comes, here it comes..."

"What? What?"

"The emotion, the trapped Qi. It's coming up and being released. Can you take it for a bit longer?"

I seriously didn't know if I could, but I was determined to release my resentments, frustration, and pent up anger. I was determined to get my $105 worth of pain. Moe could beat out every hurtful word Adolfo had said that lodged in my cells. I was ready to release the words that went all the way back to the bullies in my sixth grade class that made my life hell for a year, pulling out chunks of my hair and degrading me for being different. I was committed to this healing. I wanted to let go of past pain, my brother's untimely death, bad choices in relationships, missing my deceased father, spiteful judgments of my shallow clients, and guilt over unsaved money over the years. *Let it ALL come up and be released, yes, come...* If I didn't pass out first.

When the tapping was over, I let out a sigh of relief. I felt triumphant. I might as well have climbed Mount Everest. I made it through.

Dr. Moe instructed me to turn onto my stomach so that he could apply a few suction cups on my back. Well, heck. Gwynneth Paltrow had done it. I guessed I could, too. He left the room while I took off my shirt and bra, and I lay on my stomach in just my panties. Dr. Moe began to attach the cups. I didn't realize that they were basically "screwed" on.

It was a tad uncomfortable, but after what I went through with the beating, I didn't complain. Once the cups were all screwed on, about a half a dozen of them, Dr. Moe said, "Well, are we going to go all the way?"

Jeez! Didn't he realize I was a married woman? I looked into his eyes to see if something sadistic or perverted hid in his expression. No, not that I could tell. Then, I noticed the little demonic black wormy things swimming in their jar.

Oh.... "You mean... the leeches?"

"Yes, give it a try. Leech therapy is very effective. The leeches secrete an anti-coagulant substance from their saliva. This action allows for toxic blood to pass freely in order for the free-flow of Qi to occur."

I hesitated for a minute, wondering if I could handle having one of those creatures sucking my blood. At least, I wouldn't be able to see anything since I was lying on my stomach. And if Demi Moore could do it—which she did—so could I. They don't call LA "LA-LA-land" for nothing. And we are proud denizens.

"Go for it, Moe!" The blood-sucking had better be included in the original fee, I mentally groused.

Dr. Moe gave me an enthusiastic, "Okay, then!" and fished a leech out of the glass jar. I felt the wetness of the creature as Dr. Moe gave it a slow tour of my shoulder blade area.

"Hmm...the little guy doesn't seem to want to attach here. There is no bad blood to suck." He moved the critter down to my upper hip and the thing sank its teeth in.

"Okay, he found some!"

"How does the leech know which blood is bad?" I asked.

"The leeches have an agreement with us, with nature. Isn't it marvelous?"

21

A vision flashed across my mind of Adolfo having me taken away in a straitjacket. *They'll have you back in no time, Marlita, you'll see. Just a few shock treatments should do the trick.*

As I lay pretty much nude on the table with the cups screwed to my back and a leech sucking blood from my ass, Dr. Moe picked up his bamboo sticks and gave me a little extra treatment on the back of my lower legs. Surprisingly, it didn't hurt, which meant there was no trauma trapped in that area.

"This must be what S & M is like," I mused.

Dr. Moe laughed. "You're probably right."

When I finished, I exited the room and spotted Jason still sitting with his buddies. He shot me a crooked smile and a nod of both commiseration and congratulations. *You made it through! Awesome!*

At the cash register Dr. Moe suggested a few herbs that would assist the cleansing process. Still under the euphoria of having survived, I agreed to purchase the four bottles of liquid magic, for an extra $75 and also made a second appointment for another session of the percussion therapy.

"It can take up to five or six sessions, depending on how deep the trauma is," he explained.

I figured this wouldn't be a one shot deal. But I was in for the long haul. "I will be here, Dr. Moe."

Thinking that Julie could really benefit from this, I called her as I drove home, excited to share my new-found modality.

Her voice over the speaker phone sounded incredulous. "Marla, are you serious? Beaten with bamboo? Now that's just crazy! You will never get me to try that."

"But Julie, honestly, yes, it hurts, I mean like a son-of-a-bitch, but it is totally worth it."

"Ok, Marla...I'm really glad that you liked it, and I hope it does something for you, but I will never let someone beat me with bamboo."

That was a Wednesday afternoon. It was now Friday, and Adolfo wouldn't be home for two more hours. After my shower, I put on PJ's that fully concealed the bruises and sipped a tea made from an herb for relaxation I bought from Moe, hoping I could delay the confrontation a little longer.

I agree bamboo beatings are not for everyone, and maybe in the end I will have wasted my money, but I could honestly say that I felt I'd accomplished something with Moe drumming and whatnot on my body. It's as if the beating broke some chains, and the suction cups and leeches were able to draw forth a more authentic me—as weird as that sounds. Maybe the procedure was actually some kind of karmic gauntlet, a rite of passage with a tremendous placebo kick in the keister more than it was a treatment with actual medical benefits. Whatever it was, I felt more empowered to cope with whatever negativity came knocking at my door.

Was that Adolfo's car pulling into the garage?

The Talking Board

"The most beautiful thing we can experience is the mysterious. It is the true source of all art and science." ~ *Albert Einstein*

Action/reaction—I got that, whether it's a law of physics or a Latin spouse. I did not delude myself into thinking that I could sidestep, tapdance, or kanoodle my way around Adolfo's reaction to the sight of my bruises from the bamboo beating. *El amor de mi vida* would definitely freak out.

I was already asleep when he got home from work that Friday night, but on my way to the shower that morning, I decided to be proactive.

"Ummm... mi amor... I have something to show you... Now pleeeease don't freak out. It's not as bad as it looks."

His sleepy eyes widened and his lips parted, the jaw ready to drop.

I slipped off my robe to reveal the Dr. Moe's multi-colored masterpiece running down my legs and hips.

"Now honey, this is actually very therapeutic. And the bruises will fade...."

He was beyond anger. He looked disgusted. "Are you out of your mind? What have you done? Who did this to you?"

"Honey," I began in my most velvety tone, "this is something that I needed after all of our arguments and stress." I explained the procedure and how therapeutic it was. "Painful yes, but—"

"Just how much did you pay for this torture?"

I shaved the price down to what I paid before the extras.

"ONE HUNDRED AND FIVE DOLLARS! This guy is laughing all the way to the bank! Do NOT go back again. Look at yourself. Look at your beautiful body. I've never seen little broken capillaries like that. What if they don't go back to the way they were? You could be damaged for life!"

"I already made a second appointment." This was a boundary that only I was in charge of. He needed to respect my personal rights. "If I quit now, the results won't be nearly as effective. I AM going back. It's my money and my choice. And, of course the bruises will fade, otherwise do you think Dr. Moe would have repeat clients and all of the amazing testimonials?"

"I've heard enough! Marlita, you are NOT going back, and this spiritual bullshit better stop. You are going WAY overboard on all of this. Have you forgotten our tax audit? How will you pay your half of our back taxes?"

This stung a bit. Poor Adolfo had been stressed out for weeks, preparing all of the papers, tracking down receipts, identifying checks, deposits, and transfers that went into our accounts *three years ago.*

"How are we going to pay off our house, let alone save for retirement?" He was barely restraining a yell. "If we can't pay our mortgage, Dr. Moe doesn't care! If we have to retire in poorhouse, Dr. Moe doesn't care! Promise me that you are going to lay off this New Age stuff."

I was standing on the bath mat, nude, attempting to look sane and dignified as I offered a good rebuttal, but since none of my other arguments had worked, I changed tactics. If I couldn't be myself and keep my husband's love, then there was only one alternative: deception.

"Okay, Adolfo, you're right. I'll take a break for a while..."

"Marlita?" He knew this was too easy.

"I promise..."

I kept my promise...pretty much. After an afternoon of intense effort in matchmaking, I had actually located a colleague's client, a woman who'd done some arty semi-nude modeling. Right there on the Internet, the woman displayed the desired nipple size my Dallas client had so arrogantly specified. I, of course, wasn't going to say, *Hey, Tex, I found the nips you're after* since I made it clear I don't condone such anatomical specificity. I simply offered the connection as if I hadn't seen the pointers in question, and then he'd be pleasantly surprised sooner or later if things went well. So, I'd earned my pay and was feeling entitled to decide for myself how to spend it. Besides, tonight's foray into the phantom world wasn't going to cost anything at all.

Adolfo was working that night, so I arranged for Julie to come over at 8:00. I meditated to clear my head from Texans, tits, and tirades from Adolfo. I lit candles, burned incense, and played New Age music softly.

Julie arrived promptly at eight. Macie greeted her with lots of tail wagging and running back and forth in excitement. Julie offered her newly acquired divination tools, not one, but two talking boards that she downloaded, printed, and bonded onto foam core.

"Julie, these are great! One is gorgeous, the other so whimsical."

If Adolfo were here, he'd think we were about to use a Ouija Board. *Dios mio!* he would say. What if a demon showed up and took over our bodies?

Julie and I were just getting started in our adventures together, so we weren't concerned about that at the time.

A little background: *Ouija* is the trademarked name of William Fuld's most famous product. The generic terms for this type of divination device are: *talking board, spirit board,* and *communication board.* Since *Ouija* is the oldest known brand name, most folks erroneously refer to all talking boards as *Ouija* like calling all photocopiers *Xeroxes* or all tissues *Kleenex.* Talking boards are one modality used for *divination.* Other modalities include the casting of Runes, peering into a scrying glass, throwing bones (dice), reading tea leaves or Tarot cards, visiting the Oracle of Delphi, astrology, or simple meditation. Humans have attempted to receive messages from the beyond since the beginning of time, nothing new here. Julie and I don't agree on everything, but one thing that we both believe is that there *is* life after life and that our peeps are over there on the other side waiting to give us a message.

The only time that I knew I had a contact from the other side was over a decade ago, a few days after my father died. He had cancer, and it was an absolutely devastating experience for both of us. I moved back from Chicago to California to be with him and was by his side in the hospital while he was dying. The lowest point in my life was the day I went to the crematorium to pick up his ashes. I stored the heavy box that contained the cremains in the back of the closet at my aunt's house where I was temporarily staying. That night, lying in bed, the inside of my right ear began to buzz. I heard my dad's voice. "We did all right, didn't we? I love you." His words seemed to pass over me. "I love you, too," I said. There was so much I wanted to ask him, but I knew he was gone. I'd been to psychics, but I couldn't help but wonder if we each hold the power to contact spirits directly, especially those souls that care about us.

Since neither Julie nor I had ever used a talking board before, we were incredibly excited, but at the same time, neither of us really expected anything to happen. Julie and I were both fans of getting psychic readings, but this was totally unchartered waters.

Our *kundalini* energy was newly rising, chakras just beginning to balance, our third eyes starting to open. We were peering into portals and not sure how the spirit world might interface with the human world, but we did know that our positive intentions would shield us. I later discovered that it's important to do a ritual of protection before beginning each session.

Following me into the kitchen, Julie glanced around uneasily.

"Relax, Adolfo's at work," I said.

"Thank God, because I know he would NOT approve of this, Marla."

"Oh, I know. Especially if he saw this." I held up the whimsical witchy board.

She giggled. "Well, I had both boards made because I figure that dark board is more my personality. The white board is more you."

I opened the fridge, grabbed two mason jars of green juice, and offered one to Julie. She rolled her eyes and pulled a can of Diet Coke from her purse.

"Okay, well, maybe next time..." I wasn't giving up hope that Julie would kick her diet soda habit one day. I took a healthy verdant sip. "Mmmmmmmmm, that's good!" Julie stared at me, deadpan. "Marla. Please."

I had to laugh.

In my office/sanctuary, we chose the white board, settled on the floor, and placed the board between us. In addition to the candles surrounding the board, I placed a crystal at each corner and a statuette of Jesus, Saint Charbel, and Mother Mary. Macie came in and sat next to me. Ever curious, she always has to be part of whatever is going on.

I recited a prayer of protection and invitation:

I declare that this room, this house and this property is surrounded by the white light of Christ. Only those beings of the highest vibration, love and light are allowed here. We look forward to communication and welcome any high vibrational beings that would like to come through and give us a message.

"Oh, I almost forgot," Julie said. "I brought this." She pulled out a small green spool-like game piece to use as a planchette and set it in the middle of the board. We both placed an index finger on it.

I breathed in deeply and asked, "Is there anyone here that would like to communicate with us?"

We were so quiet I thought I heard our hearts beating. A minute went by, then another. At the three-minute mark, we gave each other the maybe-we-should-give-up look just before the planchette started to move.

"What the... OH. MY. GOD. IT'S MOVING!" I squealed.

This was thrilling to me, but Julie looked completely nonplussed, like it was an everyday occurrence. I was intrigued to find out whose energy was moving the little green piece as it spelled out H-E-L-L-O.

Julie and I simultaneously replied, "hello."

"May I ask to whom we are speaking?" I asked.

S-E-C-R-E-T.

"Are you a spirit?"

Y-E-S.

"Do you have a name?

Y-E-S.

"Will you tell us?"

N-O.

"Why not?"

F-O-R M-E.

Julie laughed. "That is hilarious. Great sense of humor!"

I continued. "Okaaaay...well, do you just want to be called Secret Spirit then?"

Y-E-S.

"Are you evil?"

N-O.

"Are you a good Spirit?"

Y-E-S.

"Do you love us?"

Y-E-S.

"What are you doing here?"

W-A-T-C-H-I-N-G.

"Watching us?

Y-E-S.

"Do you protect us?"

Y-E-S.

"Ok, well, it's nice to meet you, Secret Spirit."

G-O-O-D-B-Y-E.

Julie and I were dumbfounded, but I managed to end the session. "Thank-you, Spirit, for sharing your energy with us. We are grateful for this exchange. We now close this sacred space and surround ourselves with love and healing light."

We had actually communed with a spirit. We sat in silence before Julie finally said, "Well, he was pretty nice."

The next night would be a full moon, and we agreed to meet again.

For our second communication, we decided to use the Dark Board. Its cartoonish spooky design sent a delightful tingle up my spine. After opening the space with a protection prayer, we each put our index finger on the planchette. It started to move right away this time.

H-E-L-L-O.

I led again as the main speaker.

"Hello. With whom do we have the pleasure of speaking?"

S-E-C-R-E-T.

"Oh, hello Secret Spirit. Good to talk to you again. Do you have a message for us?"

N-Y-C. S-O-O-N.

Julie and I exchanged knowing looks. I planned to go to New York in a couple of months for a matchmaking conference.

G-O-O-D T-R-I-P.

"Thanks, Secret Spirit. Yes, I am going to New York. I am so excited. Will you tell us your name this time?"

S-E-C-R-E-T.

"Ok, well, is there anyone else here that would like to make a connection?"

The planchette remained still for a minute and then began moving again.

H-E-L-L-O.

"Hello," Julie and I replied.

"Who is this?" I asked.

A-N-G-E-L.

"Angel? You're an angel???"

Y-E-S. G-U-A-R-D-I-A-N A-N-G-E-L.

"My angel?" I asked.

Y-E-S.

"What is your name?"

M-E-R-T-H-Y-R.

"Merthyr?"

"Google it," Julie said.

I picked up my phone and searched for the word *Merthyr*. The word *merthyr* means *martyr* in old Welsh. It sort of made sense to me that my guardian angel would have that name—something to do with the way I feel about women burned at the stake for witchcraft when they were just psychic or herbalists.

"Merthyr, does your name mean martyr?"

Y-E-S.

"Where did you get that name?"

U-N-K-N-O-W-N.

"How long have you been my angel?"

A-L-W-A-Y-S.

"Will you be with me after I die?"

Y-E-S.

"What do you look like?"

I A-M T-A-L-L.

"I wish I could see you."

S-O-O-N. Y-O-U W-I-L-L S-E-E M-E. I L-O-V-E Y-O-U M-A-R-L-A.

I felt her love envelope me. Tingles ran up and down my spine. "I love you too, Merthyr."

I never imagined that I would ever get to talk to my guardian angel, at least while I was still in a body. I have always had angels decorating my house and had a great curiosity when I would hear people like Doreen Virtue speak about angels. But I was skeptical about their communication. I mean...really? How is that possible? It was a sweet sentiment, but in the back of my mind, I thought there was a possibility that these so-called angel communicators were a bit delusional. But this was real. Merthyr IS real. Julie and I were too surprised to be making this stuff up. Neither of us was making the planchette move.

We closed the session and moved into the kitchen, excited. We celebrated with different kind of spirits—shots of tequila. Using the stepladder, I climbed up to access the cupboard above the stove and selected one of Adolfo's most expensive bottles. I carefully poured us both a shot into colorful glasses Adolfo and I had bought in Puerto Vallarta. Julie and I clinked our glasses together.

"Here's to Secret Spirit," Julie said.

"Here's to Merthyr," I added. My drink brought a lovely instant warmth.

"Ahhh. Sure beats the hell out of your green juice," Julie said. "Hey, Marla, seems like Adolfo would be thrilled that you now have a direct line to Merthyr and Secret Spirit since you don't need to pay for psychic sessions or angel readings anymore. You can do them yourself."

"Yeah," I said. "I definitely need to be more frugal. Especially now."

"Oh?"

"We have to see the IRS agent tomorrow. I'm really nervous."

Julie took the liberty of refilling our glasses. "You'd better bring Merthyr along..." She took another swig. "But this may not be the best time to mention her to Adolfo."

"Especially if things don't go well," I said. I had reason to be nervous. All that lovely abundance I'd been working on could vanish in an instant.

Bring On The Blue

*"The only difference between a taxman and a taxidermist is that the
taxidermist leaves the skin."* ~ *Mark Twain*

In one hour, Adolfo and I would face the dreaded IRS in an
audit. I entered my office/spiritual sanctuary to calm myself. A disaster with numbers, I proved useless when Adolfo
assigned me the task of printing out all of the pertinent
bank statements and highlighting relevant transactions. In
fact, I threw up my hands and cried. Numbers have always
given me brain damage, causing me to flunk math classes.
Thrice. He calmly shouldered the entire burden of docu-
mentation. For this, I was and am eternally grateful.

That morning, however, I was more than a little freaked
out. I figured that fifteen minutes of meditation would help
to get me centered for what we were about to face.

I was almost into my right-brain theta-wave meditation zone—or something like that—when Adolfo yelled that

it was time to go. My head was so *not* where Goddess Tauheedah would want it to be. So, after a stop at Starbucks, I was still trying to finish my meditation in the car, focusing on deep breathing with lovely images of my angels in my head.

Adolfo interrupted my thoughts. "I'm sure we're going to end up owing some money. Now remember, Marlita, Everardo will do most of the talking. And me, of course." Translation: Don't even clear your throat as if to speak.

"You're going to need every penny. It's a good thing you cancelled that second appointment with that sadistic witch doctor. Over a hundred dollars for bullshit." He held his right hand up, palm facing me. "I am trying to be more understanding of your interests, but we could have a serious IRS problem. So please, mi amor, understand what I am trying to tell you. Don't fall for everything you hear about. It scared the shit out of me when I saw those bruises on you. Your beautiful ivory skin! You could be scarred for life. I love you and the thought of you getting beaten makes me see red."

At that instant, Adolfo slammed on the brakes. My neck snapped, and my vanilla soy latte sloshed, splattering onto my lap. Adolfo swore at the image in the rearview mirror as I shrieked. Milky coffee had seeped into my dress, leaving a caramel-colored splotch. Damn, another dry-cleaning bill.

"That asshole is tailgating me!" Adolfo hissed.

"Just move over! Let him *pass!*"

"Shut *UP!*" Adolfo bellowed as he pumped the brake. Tailgating was a crime not to go unpunished by the proud man driving our salsa red Toyota Scion.

Another lurch.

More coffee spilled, and I screamed, "WHAT IN THE HELL IS GOING ON?"

As if in answer to my frantic query, the tailgater darted into the lane to our left, accelerated with a roar, cut in front of us, and slammed on HIS brakes.

I screamed louder. "OH, MY GOD! WE ARE GOING TO DIE!"

"Stop screaming!" Adolfo's middle finger articulated his disdain for his new enemy. He switched lanes, hit the gas, and pulled alongside the culprit.

"Fucking ASSHOLE!"

He yelled so loudly, I would have feared ruptured vocal cords—he's a musician who sings as he plays the piano—if my life hadn't been passing in front of me, preparing me for eternity.

More revs and lurches.

"You're playing CHICKEN on the FREEWAY?" I was still shrieking. "Oh, my God! What is the matter with you? STOP IT!"

"Shut up! I know what I'm doing."

I was hyperventilating. Thankfully, the tailgater took the next exit and disappeared as quickly as he came, a storm of fury, fueled by ego, pride, and testosterone—very much like that of my husband's, actually. Even though I did promise Adolfo that I would not go back for more beatings, I was certain that some stress and trauma were released in that one powerful session. Now, I could feel the toxic load percolating right back into my cells.

Perfect. Our audit should go smoothly indeed.

I gulped the remainder of my rapidly cooling latte, grateful to live another day. I could make myself as mellow as all get-out, but I still have to deal with testosterone poisoning all too often. It was like a tornado that sucked me into its funnel of fury. This wasn't the first incidence of road rage emanating from my adoring husband. The most memorable one was on the way to church one Sunday. It was speed up-slam on brakes- yell-cuss-flip the bird-damn near crash, and then peace-be-with-you, all within a twenty-minute stretch.

Fragments of a proctologist joke came to mind, something about the first couple of probes shocking the bejesus out of him, but soon the assholes made up just another day at the office. So, though I was indeed shaken, I wasn't totally surprised. I had heard that high levels of testosterone increase men's sense of pride and boost self-image—which may be fine for the testy, hormone-rich male, but it didn't do much for me.

We arrived in tact at our destination, the location of another sort of "tailgater," the IRS. Despite the freeway drama, we were early, and Adolfo bought me an instant coffee from a food truck across the street—all the apology I would receive. I could have used a shot of tequila, but even that wouldn't erase my exasperation.

We located the office in the back of the two-story building and waited in the tiny lobby for our taxman, Everardo. Adolfo calmly thumbed through an old issue of *National Geographic*. He looked up at me, smiling, completely at ease.

"How is your coffee, mi amor?"

It's speeding all the adrenaline in my system to my extremities, preparing me for fight or flight, and I can't stop quivering, I wanted to say, but I just shook my head. I let drama affect me. When you receive energies, subtle or blatant, from someone else's emotions, the aural body reacts as well as the physical one, as Tauheedah explained. Chakra openings, powerful yet vulnerable, swirl with the energies and can distribute them into your more vulnerable areas. "If there is a hole in the aura, low energy beings can attach themselves," Tauheedah said, "especially at the tailbone." I admit it sounded like something out of a B horror movie, but Tauheedah was wiser than I knew at the time. I wasn't taking any chances. I'd be balancing my chakras first chance I got.

Everardo arrived, carrying a manila envelope. He greeted me with a friendly smile and a handshake and sat next to Adolfo. They chatted in Spanish and shuffled through the files. Things were more complicated than usual, since the tax year in question was when one of our dreams came true. We had saved like misers and finally purchased our first home.

I sipped the last of my coffee as Janelle, our assigned tax auditor, called us into her office. I silently recited a few prayers to Merthyr, asking for any assistance she could give us, as Janelle dug into our file and went through our deposits one by one. We received a summary in the mail a couple of weeks prior that totally had our chakras spinning in the wrong direction. Janelle must have flunked math classes as I did since she came to the conclusion that we owed almost a half a million dollars. Gasp. Choke. We pointed out that many of the deposits she was referring to were transfers from online savings accounts to make the down payment on the house. NOT income!

After an hour and a half of what felt like Chinese water torture, we trudged, defeated, back to our car. We still owed $23,000.

Adolfo ran his hands through his hair. "Shit!"

We were blindsided and quiet.

I looked at my watch. "We need to beat the traffic."

I mentioned my class at The Imagine Center. I was meeting Julie at 6:00 PM. It was our first class of a series of six on "manifesting," called, "Dream Weaver."

"Marlita, mi amor, you shouldn't be spending money..." he scolded.

His nerves were now even more on edge than mine, so I managed to convince him with some gentle caresses and sweet talk that I really needed to go to my class tonight to diffuse all of the negativity that the IRS had bestowed upon us, and coax my energy back in the right direction. I tried to see the day as my opportunity to prove to Adolfo that this manifestation stuff worked.

"And darling," I reasoned, "the cost is only 15.00 per class. Hardly enough to put us further in debt."

Dreading maneuvering in the tiny back lot, I managed to find a prime spot in front of the Imagine Center. *Hey, your luck is turning already, Marla*, said a perky little voice from within.

Before stepping out of the car, I closed my eyes and breathed deeply. Then, once inside the retail part of the center, I thumbed through a book on astral travel as Julie arrived, a whirling dervish of outrage and angst. Her aquamarine eyes were wild, and her hands gestured in wide arcs. She exclaimed in a stage whisper, "MARLA!!!! YOU WON'T BELIEVE WHAT JUST HAPPENED!"

"Oh, boy....."

"I just had a fight with a guy in the parking lot!"

"What do you mean a fight? What guy?"

"No-no-no... I am serious! It almost came to blows! This A-hole told me I couldn't park back there. He was saving spaces with orange cones. *What the hell?* I told him I'm a customer here, and I could park wherever I wanted. And he should go F himself!"

I gasped.

"Then he lunged at me! I *almost* smacked him, but I controlled myself. After all, this is a spiritual center."

"Come here." I led her to a shelf offering an array of cobalt blue spray bottles. I selected the healing aura cleansing spray that contained ten organic essential oils, blessed and made during the summer solstice.

"Close your eyes and take a deep breath." I spritzed her aura from head to toe. "You need some serious clearing and balancing, girl!"

Julie giggled as I turned her around to spritz her back as well. "Who else but me would get into a parking lot brawl at a spiritual center?"

Hmmmm... I could think of one other person. It is said that souls come together to learn a lesson or to heal something from a past life. With Adolfo I was learning patience and acceptance. Sure, it would be great if he were more like me and didn't let little things like a tailgater push him into a downward spiral, but, like the rest of us, he is here to learn the lessons he needs to learn.

Julie and I and the other eight students, all women mostly of Hispanic heritage, settled into our seats in the back room. The vibration was so high and peaceful, that I immediately felt the tension lift from my shoulders. I'd gotten to know my classmates enough to know that we were all here to experience a breakthrough. We all knew that there was a higher self, awaiting a shift in consciousness, spiritual power, and enlightenment.

With her usual commanding and graceful energy, Goddess Tauheedah sat down in front of the class. After a group prayer, calling in our spirit guides and angels, she explained that dream weaving is about mastering energy and that we needed a dream to manifest. This isn't just about getting a new car or winning the lottery. This dream must be something fulfilling and important, something that touches others with beauty.

"The divine gifts that you hold become your beauty," she said.

I looked over at Julie. As a ghostwriter, her divine gift is helping others tell their story. She brings out their beauty while shining in her own way. I mentally sent warm glittery vibes toward her. I know that my divine gift is playing Cupid, shooting my arrows of love, hoping one will reach its target once in a while. Witnessing a couple fall in love because of me, that feels fulfilling and important. Yet my dream involves self-realization as well. This entails understanding my free will, willpower, and voice. In the beginning was the Word.

"Watch what you speak," Tauheedah said, "for it begins the manifestation process." With her bejeweled hands, she gestured toward her throat. "In this session, we are focusing on the throat chakra. The throat, or (fifth) chakra, starts at the hollow point of the neck where our voice conveys our will. This blue chakra holds the matrix for what we want to manifest."

It is the field of manifest dreams, she told us. We can sense our destiny through the throat chakra.

Amazingly, this felt profoundly true to me. I experienced that sensation of revealing to myself what I already knew. And my destiny was taking shape to the extent that I knew when I was moving toward it instead of floundering around, missing it. During that two-hour class, I could feel a definite shift take place. The IRS didn't hold a candle to the power in that room. My guides were with me; Merthyr was with me, and together we held the power to manifest whatever was needed. I had already come across the definition of abundance given by Bashar—an entity channeled by Darryl Anka:

"ABUNDANCE: *the ability to do what you need to do when you need to do it.*"

I loved that. And I was eager to do the homework Tauheedah gave us:

"Craft your dream and map your dream," she said. "Lay your vision on your altar by placing a clear quartz crystal and a blue stone on a money bill. For mindfulness, wear blue for the next two weeks. The more blue energy that we bring in, the more volume we bring in. Light a blue candle every day and meditate on it."

Oh, yes, I will do this. I was actually acquiring skills that I had admired in others and wondered why they had a direct line to the mystical, which seemed to be an unlisted number. Now, I thought...I just may be entering the same area code.

Abundance, Astral Travel, and the Sound of One Hand Slapping A Thigh

"The soul is motivated for one thing, to make us whole again."
~ Teal Swan

Tauheedah said that we needed to map our dream and craft our dream so that it may manifest. I had to think about that as I drove home. Of course I wanted abundance, who didn't? Yet I felt like I'd been nudging a sleeping genie, a soul connection to the universe, and I wanted more. In fact, what I felt was like a ravenous hunger as if I'd been starving all my life and had glimpsed a banquet on a golden table set with silver and crystal. I wanted abundant joy and love and freedom. How could I "map" that? I wanted to become whole, a fully realized life form of Source, filled with connection and understanding and magnificence. I didn't quite know how to "craft" all that, but I wouldn't let that stop me. And I could simply focus on one thing at a time...

When I got home from class, I pulled out a beautiful silk scarf that I bought in Paris years ago and wrapped it around my neck. With royal, azure, and turquoise running through it, I figured it should cover the whole blue spectrum for the power of manifestation. I cleared the books from two of the shelves of the tall, cherry wood bookcase and carefully dedicated a new altar for this purpose specifically, adding my magical doodads. A green candle stood on the middle shelf, along with a hundred dollar bill—green for abundance. On top of the bill, I arranged small stones of lapis lazuli, jade, citrine, and green aventurine. I needed all available help, so my statuettes of Catholic saints collected over the years from my trips to Mexico City, Jesus, Mary, St. Charbel, St. Martin de Porres, and Saint Jude joined the party. I added my little bottle of green anointing oil (for prosperity) made by the Lucky Mojo Curio Company and added a large pinecone dipped in gold glitter and a ceramic skull painted in purples and greens that I bought on a trip to Cozumel.

I sat in front of the altar on my sparkly meditation pillow in colors of blue, purple, and gold and made in India— Thank you, Ross. If my plans worked out, my pillows and I wouldn't need to dress for less. I rubbed some oil onto the candles, lit them, and recited my abundance affirmations:

Infinite Spirit, open the way for my great abundance. I am an irresistible magnet for all that belongs to me by Divine Right.

Unexpected doors fly open; unexpected channels are free, and endless avalanches of abundance are poured out upon me, under grace in perfect ways.

Manifest! Manifest, golden light! Bring me my divine birthright.

I also said a prayer that a stressful legal battle I had gotten myself into with someone over the rights to one of my creative projects would be settled. My attorney had been back and forth with this person for months, but they were determined to hang on, possibly out of spite, I wasn't exactly sure. All I knew was that I wanted out of the contract and be free to shop my project around Hollywood unfettered.

I went to bed, offering joyful appreciation for the bounty headed my way, unaware that my next spiritual breakthrough would soon occur.

After a restful sleep, I woke and couldn't dip back into slumber. I imagined the time at about 8:30 AM, judging by the late fall morning light slipping in through the blinds. I heard birds happily chirping outside the sliding glass door where I'd set up a feast of bird seed, dried corn kernels also for the squirrels, sunflower seeds, peanuts in the shell, and a dish of water on our weathered wooden café table.

Beside me, Adolfo snored lightly. The house was glacial, and I didn't feel like getting up yet, so I snuggled under the covers with headphones in my ears as I listened on my iPhone to one of my favorite spiritual teachers, Teal Swan, talk about the psychology of projecting one's expectations onto another person. Teal says that our romantic partners tend to be our opposing mirror and any extreme aversion to a trait in another person is a reflection of the level of rejection we have developed toward that trait or its potential within ourselves. Teal also says that the more we love something in someone else, the more we have denied it in ourselves, probably during childhood or adolescence. I could see how I have always been so drawn to people with intuitive and healing abilities and the correlation of how I'd turned away from listening to my own intuition for most of my life. Somewhere along the line, I'd started turning off the still small voice and had plunged into behaviors based on hormones or some social value, leading to behaviors that put me in compromising positions with men that literally could have gotten me raped or even killed.

Weirdly, my body began to vibrate, as if a motor switched on in the mattress, only there was no such motor. OMG! YES! I knew what was happening. Not only had I read about astral projection in my handy *Astral Travel for Beginners* guide, purchased at the Imagine Center, I'd actually experienced it numerous times as a child. It usually would happen in the summertime on a hot day. The heat often made me lethargic, so I'd lie on my bed, but then I'd feel a sudden vibrating sensation and a feeling of being pulled up and out of my body. Once I, or rather my astral spirit, sat in the corner of the bedroom, watching my body. It freaked me out, causing me to snap back inside myself.

The scariest experience occurred one night when I was asleep and awoke, startled to feel my soul/spirit being pulled up in a way that was different from the other experiences. This time it felt like someone or something was pulling me out of my body. I was scared shitless, and I pulled back with all of my might, literally fighting for my soul, not sure if I would win the battle. Whatever was pulling me, finally let go. To this day, I have no idea what that was about.

I now felt confident and grounded in my faith and spiritual growth, compared to when I was a kid, and now my sense of spiritual experimentation beckoned. I decided to go with it. Nothing to be afraid of...Just relax, I told myself.

I didn't want my headphones to hinder an astral adventure, but just as I began to raise my hands towards my ears, they dropped to my sides. I was paralyzed. Yet, I lifted up out of my body. To my left, just beyond Adolfo, I saw two images out of the corner of my eye—my astral eye. Two translucent white beings walked by. I was seeing beyond the thin veil, something I'd only dreamed of doing. In fact, a multitude of spirits, beings, and angels were around us. They must be here all the time, I thought. Most of us can't see them, including me. I was shocked but also thrilled.

"Go! Fly! It's okay! YES!" I told myself. I felt myself lifting up... up... up... Holy crap! *I am flying...*

...I saw millions of beautiful stars lit against a black sky. I was in outer space. This was crazy! As I got closer, the stars came into view more clearly. It was so quiet and peaceful. I had never been anywhere so magical. Suddenly, I was traveling fast. I was flying closer to earth and water came into view. It was the most beautiful transparent, sparkling blue ocean. I passed over some villas with reddish rooftops that were perched on a hill above the water until I was hovering over the ocean. It looked like I was somewhere in the Mediterranean, possibly Greece. I felt overwhelmed by the beauty. The earth was exquisite! I was moving quickly again, this time I hovered above the ground, which was covered in snow. I headed towards a building that appeared to be a barn or storage space. I noticed that someone was off to my right and holding my hand. This was strange, why was someone holding my hand? The person moved in front of me and led me towards the building. We were walking on the snow. I could only see the back of him, but my intuition told me it was Jesus. His hair came just to the nape of his neck and was a light brown. Somehow I thought his hair would be longer, as he is depicted in paintings. Before we reached the building, we turned and headed toward an embankment. I was standing on the ground trying to climb up and over it, but it was a challenge. Why wasn't I flying?

I made it over the top...

And then I was back in my body.

Damn, that was quick. I wanted to stay longer. I took the headphones out of my ears, and snuggled deep under the covers, wanting to relish my experience. I heard Adolfo get up and start dressing next to the bed. I pretended I was still asleep and finally opened my eyes again at 10:00 AM. Adolfo had opened the blinds. Still lying in bed, I looked out through the sliding glass door at the red blossoms of the bougainvillea cascading over the brick wall into our yard. The sun was shining, birds chirping. What a beautiful day!

I showered and dressed leisurely, thrilled with the magic of adjustable water temperature and fluffy towels. It felt so good to be alive. I hummed as I made the bed and then went to the kitchen and made Macie an extra special breakfast with some of the steak Adolfo had brought home from work and mixed it in with her canned food. Then I retrieved my Breville juicer out of the cupboard.

I fed in five kinds of organic vegetables, plus fresh ginger and lemon, feeling completely rooted in my power. As I poured my heavenly elixir—what Julie calls green gunk— into a mason jar, the phone rang. It was my favorite new client, Jeremy, a sensitive novelist and dad of two girls. Jeremy was not only a great catch and easy to match because of his creative career and good looks, but he was seriously the most low-maintenance client I'd ever had. He never got snippy or demanding, and actually felt terrible for turning down an introduction once in a while, in contrast to Steven, a spine surgeon in San Diego, who had turned down 30 women's profiles in two months' time. I took my juice into my office and closed the door, ready to give Jeremy my full attention as he recounted his experience with the latest gal I'd set him up with, Miranda.

"Miranda and I have seen each other about eight times now." He sounded nervous. "We went away for the weekend to Santa Barbara and had an incredible time. I am so attracted to her, that I find it hard to be away from her. And I know that she feels the same about me. We literally want to be together all the time."

"But..." I wanted to be thrilled, but there was no joy in his voice. "There is a problem..."

"Yes."

Silence. Possible scenarios ran through my brain. Gawd... maybe she asked him to buy her an expensive handbag, like some of the gold-diggers did, or even worse, asked to borrow money. I'd had a feeling Miranda was this sort of young woman, but she was otherwise such a sweet girl with a natural beauty and very likable.

"Jeremy?"

"Yes. Well...Miranda confessed that she is a sugarbaby."

I had heard of this term and learned of a website that offers young women connections with men willing to pay for "an arrangement." This could mean spending two nights a week with him, escorting him to events, traveling, or just getting together for sex. A bargain is made that involves compensation in the form of jewelry, cars, debt coverage, or anything they choose, including, presumably, cash.

"Uh-oh..."

"Yeah. She said that she wants to stop and find true love, but she needs to do some more deals to make her financial goal of having a million dollars in the bank. Honestly, Marla, the thought of her having sex with other men makes me nuts. She says that it is 'just business,' but really? Imagine if I married her, what would I tell my kids? Yes, my sweeties, your new stepmother works nights. Why? Oh, she has sex with other men, but no big deal, it's just business."

"Dear god, Jeremy." I felt devastated. I could tolerate fussy clients, but not this. My worst nightmare was inadvertently introducing my client to someone who would break his or her heart or incur financial disaster or...*please don't let this be the case*...both.

"I know I don't make enough money for her, Marla. She was upset with me and wouldn't speak to me for a week because I wouldn't buy her a new refrigerator. She feels that I need to step up financially and take care of things like this for her," he said.

So there it was, the double whammy of heartbreak and exploitation. I spoke with Jeremy for an hour, letting him pour his heart out as he recounted conversations and possible outcomes.

Afterward, I wondered what Teal Swan would say about this horrible attraction? Possibly that Jeremy had chosen a path of honoring his talent and self-expression over simple earning power and projected the abandoned side of himself onto the woman he was attracted to. And Miranda had chosen a path that honored her allure and earning power, totally abandoning the authentic side of herself that might have unique talents which could actually provide the abundance she craved. That was probably oversimplifying things, but I sensed it was part of the smoke and ash that rose out of a fiery love.

I wished that Miranda could experience a spiritual breakthrough and feel what it was like to fly among the stars. The beauty of the Universe is so expansive, powerful, magical and incredible. Life is worth more than piling money in the bank at whatever cost, whether it was selling your body, your time, or your soul. I felt compassion for her. To live in such fear that she felt her only salvation lay in using men for her own advancement suggested a challenging childhood and lack of love. But I also felt so sad for Jeremy, finding a girl that he thought he clicked with and desired, only to be forced to face his financial shortcomings.

I messed up. I had not done my due diligence in checking this girl out. She hadn't revealed this little tidbit about herself, but would I have to hire a detective? Should I give my clients a warning statement? The Surgeon General has determined that use of this dating service might be dangerous to your heart.

Self-blame began to snowball. Even before Tauheedah, I'd been working on manifesting abundance. Was this current disaster a be-careful-what-you-wish-for situation? Was I going to have to stipulate in my prayers and affirmations and incantations that no harm should come in the process of supplying my abundance?

Wait a minute.

We're here on this planet to work out just such issues. Perhaps I simply hastened a dynamic that needed balancing for both Jeremy and Miranda. But did that make it okay? The whole evolution of life depended on predators learning to outsmart prey and the herbivores developing strategies for thriving despite the entities that wanted to devour them. This was why primates stopped walking on their forelimbs and grew bigger brains and figured out how to manage fire and wheels and such. Disaster is an opportunity for growth; I get that, but I did not want to be an exploitive catalyst.

So where did that put me? Jeez.

I think if I listened closely, I might have heard the sound of one hand slapping Buddha's portly thigh as he got in a good belly laugh.

The Pendulum

"The pendulum of the mind alternates between sense and nonsense, not between right and wrong." ~ Carl Jung

The few months attending classes with Julie had been exhilarating. Bit by bit we were adding knowledge and tools that would always be with us. Our talking board sessions had been such a success that we were feeling quite capable and rooted in our power. Merthyr told me that I should just call her *Murth*. How adorable is that? I only wished that I could use the talking board on my own. Every time I wanted to talk with Murth, I had to call Julie and hope that she could come over. When I asked Murth why I could not use the board by myself, she answered, E-N-E-R-G-Y. And she told me that I needed to meditate more.

We were especially excited about the class we were attending that afternoon at the Green Man Store about how to use a pendulum. Julie and I each owned two pendulums, and we also co-owned one that Julie purchased at a New Age expo last month, a quartz crystal in the shape of a square. Julie said that she wasn't "feeling it" so she brought it to my house, where it happily resides in a silk purple pouch on my altar. We pretty much thought we had the hang of it as far as pendulum use goes, but we weren't sure if the information coming through was a spirit or our subconscious. And we came up with some pretty strange answers to our inquiries.

I pulled into Julie's driveway as she was walking out the door. She jumped into the passenger seat and slammed the door.

"Let's go!" she barked, shooting worried glances towards the house across the street.

"Oh no, you are NOT still in a tizzy about your neighbor, are you?"

Julie looked sheepish and let out an exasperated breath. "Ye-ehsss......"

She had broken her own rule and dated her neighbor, although *date* is probably not the most accurate term. She and Sergio were the best of buds for years, hanging together at neighborhood BBQs, watching movies at his house on his giant flat screen TV while drinking beer and shots of tequila, ribbing each other about political views, and chatting on the street corner under the moonlight while Romeo the Chihuahua did his business before bedtime. Julie had a secret crush, but kept it under wraps, since Sergio didn't seem interested in that way.

Everything was fine until a couple of months ago when Sergio invited Julie to go camping in his RV....with one bed. Blindsided, she was totally confused. Was he interested in her beyond friendship, or was this just a neighbor inviting a friend? She was too shy to ask what his motives were, so she agonized over what to do. The stakes were high since if things didn't work out, their friendship could be compromised. That would devastate her.

She decided to take the risk, and the first day things went well, including a walk on the beach and dinner around a campfire. The second night, however, a mixture of tequila, a heated political debate, and awkward sex twisted the experience into a fiasco she wanted to forget. As soon as Sergio pulled the RV into his driveway, Julie jumped out, mumbled "ummmm...well...g'-bye...." and never heard from Sergio again. Until recently.

"He's been texting me," Julie admitted.

"*Really?* What does he say? Is he sorry for the way he treated you? I mean, just to never speak to you again, that is pretty harsh!"

Julie scrunched down in the seat, motioning for me to get going. "Marla...last night he texted me a photo of his privates."

I gasped. "WHAT?" *OH MY GOD.* That was just plain crazy!

"What do you think it means?" She sat up again after we turned off of her street. "Why would he do that? Is he interested in me? I mean, why would a guy do that?"

"Well, that is so rude, Julie, I would block his number, I mean that is totally inappropriate, how gross!"

"*Really?* It would bother you if a guy sent you a text like that? I don't think it's a big deal...I just wonder what it means?"

"JULIE, if a guy *ever* sent me a photo of his junk..." Though driving, I turned to give her a meaningful look. "I would NEVER want to see him again."

Her responding expression said *are you for real?*

I didn't know what to say. Did a guy who did this stuff actually think a woman might text back praising the magnificence of his member and begging to be his sex slave? Maybe it was an easy wordless bargain, a what-the-hell kind of shot that meant *if she likes this, I can have her on my terms. No messy emotions. If not, who cared?* Was it a statement of dominance: You, bitch, are part of my big boy's turf? Or was he simply flipping her off in a highly graphic way?

I didn't want to preach or make Julie feel like I was judging her, so I just said, "I go for a more sophisticated, elegant type of man. Anthony Weiner antics are not my style AT ALL!"

"Well, we obviously have different views on *that* subject. I just want to stop thinking about him all the time. I've started drinking margaritas alone in my bedroom at night as I peek out of the blinds, staring at his house. This is plain crazy and has got to stop. I think I'm going to have Hovik dress a candle for me, one that will make me forget all about Sergio."

Hovik is a powerful warlock who works at The Green Man Store. Julie and I are in total awe of him. He dresses candles with oils, herbs, sparkles, and magical intention and incantations. Could this magic be powerful enough to override Julie's feelings for Sergio? Intentions are powerful things. Magical candles less so, but ritual can be extremely effective in reinforcing intentions and reprogramming habitual thinking. Julie's intention was stuck inside her, but if Hovik took that intention and gave it a specific candle that was just for Julie, it gave her an outward and visible form, bringing Hovik, the candle, and Julie—three focal points instead of one—into the task of forgetting Sergio.

We arrived fifteen minutes early, so Julie marched up to the apothecary in the back of the store. I felt like I'd stepped into a Harry Potter book. Hovik, thirty-something with a full head of chestnut hair, dressed in black and wore round, wooden studs in both ears. He stood behind an ornately carved wood bar. Dozens of jars filled with mysterious herbs, oils, and potions lined the shelves. Julie explained her obsession to Hovik, asking if he would *please* dress a candle for her that would make it all stop.

Hovik nodded with assurance, as if women all over Los Angeles flocked to his apothecary, attempting to forget the lovers that had spurned them. He selected a crimson candle from one of the shelves, took a sharpened stone knife and began to carve Julie's intentions into the wax.

"I'll go save us a seat," I told Julie.

At the back of the store, I parted a silky black curtain, entered a small room and scored a spot on one of the three velvet love seats placed around a large oak table. Julie soon joined me and a half a dozen other women.

The teacher, a curvaceous middle-aged witch with shoulder-length wine-colored hair, entered and began.

"Moses used a pendulum to discover water hidden in a rock," she said. The woman spoke of the many cultures using pendulums for a wide range of purposes over the millennia. Cave drawings in Algeria painted eight thousand years ago depict the use of a pendulum, and Chinese emperors used them to predict the future. Pendulums have fallen in and out of favor over the years, just like the Ouija Board, and at times were even outlawed.

There are a lot of misconceptions about pendulums. "Fears," the witch said, "make some people leery of their 'power,' but there is nothing to be afraid of. It is human energy, working in concert with the natural world that makes the pendulum swing in a magical way."

Julie and I exchanged excited glances, eager to be able to master another tool that would allow us to contact The Great Beyond.

Holding up a shimmery moonstone pendulum, the teacher continued, "You must program your pendulum before you use it. You only need to do this step once." She told us to place our feet flat on the floor, resting our elbows on the table and holding the pendulum by the end of the chain between our thumbs and index fingers. We were directed to keep the upper body and back straight so the energy could flow freely and place the other hand flat on the table.

"Relax," she said. "Let your breath flow calmly. Ask your pendulum: 'What does a *yes* look like?' then 'What does a *no* look like?' and 'what does *I don't know* look like'?"

This was basic; Julie and I had already programmed our pendulums, but we went along with the class. I was using my hexagon shaped amethyst pendulum, and Julie her teardrop shaped quartz crystal.

Some psychics—like Teal Swan—actually see thought-energy patterns in everything, flowing as if by crystalline, fractal design. As I thought about the circular *yes* pattern of my pendulum, I wondered if it might be because the energy flow around a positive outcome is like a small whirlwind, picking up the vibrations of self and also of the collective environment that happen to be in harmony with it. That might mean that if I had an energy intention that swirls clockwise, but the thoughts and obstacles around it block that flow in certain ways, the surrounding energy might create a counter-clockwise or chaotic energy flow that would cause my pendulum to swing back and forth in the straight line of no, or quiver with uncertainty.

"You can place your pendulum directly over an object and test it," the witch said. "For example, you could test your water, groceries, medications, gemstones, and herbs. You could determine what therapies are good simply by writing down the name, holding the pendulum over it, and asking. You could test the energy of your house, evaluate your sleeping space, and more."

We had fun testing our chakras and giving each other readings. I asked the pendulum about the outcome of my legal issue. Much to my disappointment, it just quivered. The rest of the class was pretty basic, but we enjoyed our afternoon.

I dropped Julie off in her driveway. She waved and scurried into the house. Before pulling away, I checked out Sergio's house. I'd never seen the hombre that had Julie in such a tailspin and was now even more curious to get a glimpse of the man that thought his penis should do his communicating for him.

After playing hooky for half the day fooling around with pendulums, I needed to get *some* work done, so I booted up my computer. One of my clients, Brian, sent me an email explaining that he wanted to put his membership on hold because he was crazy about Adrienne, a sweet Brazilian with a bod that wouldn't quit. "She is beautiful inside and out...Thanks, Marla, for all that you do. I think I have found my soul mate."

Happy dance! This was why I stayed in the matchmaking game. Occasionally, the stars aligned, and lovers connected to create a miracle.

I scrolled down and the next subject line read: *I am wondering how much for you to set me up on a coffee date with Kristen Wiig?* The email simply begged to be shared:

Hello Marla, I am 51- year- old man from Vancouver, CANADA. I'm seeking a come-hither beautiful sweet Vegan or Vegetarian that is very spiritual, authentic, adaptable, and an armpit shaver (it's just a preference). A staunch believer and understanderer (I know it's not a word, but it should be) and I was wondering, if a man speaks his mind in a forest and no woman hears him, is he still wrong?

I'm 100% vegetarian, 90% Vegan and 10% Cheeseian (some just say cheesy, but it's usually a higher percentage). I am actually looking to reduce my cheese consumption for several reasons, one of which is that it gives me gas, and a host of other things; is that too much information?

I'm a uni-tasker (much like a dog), an early bird (much like a bird), love early morning silence and am very handy (that was kinda random), speaking of random, I thoroughly enjoy random acts of kindness... I'll fill you in later.

Best of luck in your search for me, you're going to need all the help you can get... Haha? (I have a healthy fear of women).

Oh and I am currently trying to get through Curious George - The Man With the Yellow Hat...in Swahili. I think I'm so funny.

A real treasure, that one. My index finger dive-bombed onto the *delete* button.

By 10:15 that night, Adolfo was at work, and I was lying in bed, watching a rerun of Seinfeld. A text came in from Julie.

Marla, R U up?

I dialed her number. "What's going on?

She sounded a bit frantic. "Okay, I let the candle burn for the past seven hours, and now I am supposed to bury it at a crossroads...."

I turned off the TV right at the part where George's fiancée, Susan, keels over whilst licking envelopes for their wedding invitations. Julie had my full attention.

"What are you talking about?"

"Hovik told me that I needed to burn the candle for six hours straight while meditating on the outcome that I want and then bury it at a crossroads after dark."

"Does that mean an intersection? Where are you going to go?"

"I don't know. Am I just supposed to grab a shovel and dig a hole in one of my neighbor's yards?"

"Um...well..."

"I mean, what if someone comes out of the house? What do I tell them? *Oh, um... Hi, my name is Julie, and I live down the street. A warlock dressed a candle and put a spell put on it, and now I just need to bury it in your yard because you live at my nearest cross street... heh... heh...?*"

"Yeah, that sounds good. I'm sure they'd understand. The cops too."

"I'll figure something out..."

"Julie, please be careful, I mean really...don't go too far, and call me as soon as you're done..."

I was very concerned about Julie. Her antics felt familiar. I once set a guy's photo on fire and then ran over it with my car...but I was twenty-four years old at the time.

My pendulum lay beside the bed, and I gripped it, pondering Julie's emotional turmoil over her neighbor. It

61

touched a resonant chord inside me. She isn't much younger than I, and yet she had such powerful, seemingly adolescent angst over her puerile neighbor, *puerile* being a polite synonym for *immature fuckwit*. I'd like to think that if I had to date again at my age—please, universe, bring Adolfo home safely tonight and spare me that fate—I'd be able to draw on my experience and my carefully nurtured self-respect to make wonderfully mature choices. Yet, there I was in my fifth decade, dealing with so many puerile individuals with their hearts (and other anatomical parts) on the line. When it came to dating, age was no guarantee of wisdom.

I got up and braced myself correctly on the top of the dresser and held my pendulum. "Will I quit being a matchmaker soon?" I asked it.

It kept still a moment and then began to twitch, meaning *I don't know*.

As irritating as that was, I do understand that, as Teal Swan points out, the future is a blend of what has been set up in the past and of new intentions. The past creates probabilities, some of which reach the power of an oncoming tidal wave. Clairvoyants, actuaries, and other data analysts can often accurately predict such inevitabilities. Yet with the presence of powerful new ideas and plans, the thrilling possibility is born of changing destinies. I had a lot of work to do if I wanted to change mine so that the pendulum would move with the inevitability of *yes*.

The Crystalline Force

"We think we live in the world, but the world lives in us."
~ *Deepak Chopra*

I signed up for another course at the Imagine Center, one on crystal healing because I thought it sounded interesting—which is odd because up until that time, if I saw a hippie-type wearing a crystal on a chain, I never wondered if I should get one. I knew that crystals supposedly attracted a spiritual connection and held some sort of power, but I'd always pooh-poohed the idea. What could the crystal actually do just hanging around a person's neck?

The class drew me anyway, but I never thought of it as having much potential for follow-up, yet when Tauheedah told us that we could become certified as crystal healers, well, something resonated deeply. Marla Martenson, crystal healer. I let that sink into my bones, right down to my soul. It felt good. It felt right.

As the shallowness of my day-to-day job as a match-maker continued to gnaw at my spirit, I yearned to not only heal my clients, but to heal myself. I'd recently dealt with a thirty-nine-year-old client, Stuart, who had declined to meet a sweet, intelligent, beautiful gal, Samantha, because he was looking for someone "with more of a heart-shaped face." I had an initial inclination to rearrange *his* face, but then I stopped myself and sent out a prayer, an affirmation of love and acceptance. I didn't want to feel resentful any longer. I took a breath and counted my blessings. Yes, my clients were high-maintenance, but because of them, I was able not only to be my own boss and make my own schedule, but I could grab my laptop and work from anywhere in the world. One of the biggest blessings was being able to go to Seattle and stay with my mom a few times a year. My mom has a 2,000 square foot triple wide manufactured home in the suburbs of Seattle, where I grew up. There is a whole room off the side of the kitchen with a large oak table, love seat, coffee table, and beautiful art and craft items that we picked up in Tehran when we lived there in 1978. The view out of the bay window is of the park below and its majestic fir trees and grass, offering wonderful bird- and squirrel-watching, with the occasional appearance of a raccoon or fox. I loved setting up shop on the oak table whenever I was in town. How many professions could enable me to do this?

My clients also bailed me to get out of credit card debt and helped me buy a beautiful house in the valley, with a swimming pool and a fig tree. I also put some money into my retirement account and was able to go on amazing vacations every year. And now I could embark on this magical journey of self-discovery. I was pretty damn lucky, and I knew it...and yet...as a mere human, my ego didn't hesitate to make an appearance every so often, whispering in my ear, "hey Marla, why don't you just leave all this behind? Let the shallow fuckwits troll the Internet for heart-shaped faces, nickel-sized nips and rounded buttocks?"

So, as I sat there in Tauheedah's crystal class, feeling a change stirring. I certainly didn't know it at the time, but becoming a crystal healer was the beginning of a profound healing journey that would forever change me. All I knew was that I was hooked.

I had no idea that *all* stones are crystals, not just clear quartz. I'd certainly been enlightened about so many things over the last few months. There were five women including myself, in the dimly lit room. A candle flickered on a white marble table to the left of Tauheedah, casting flickering shadow against the wall. The room smelled of wild sage and incense.

I furiously took notes, not wanting to miss a word that Tauheedah said. Standing in front of a poster of the human body, she pointed to the head and explained that our pineal gland is actually a crystal, and it can communicate with all crystals. Say what? That totally blew my mind!

"There is a natural match between the human element and the crystalline force. We are in the Aquarius age now and we are in a reunification process on the planet. All stones carry a vibration, energy and consciousness."

Tauheedah picked up a large piece of rose quartz. "Pink stones are for love. Rose quartz is a stone of love and compassion and helps us express ourselves as love. Pink calcite is soothing. It draws and expels energy. It can draw out unsafe energy. When we have been burned by love, we have emotional scars around love. Our intent as healers is to hold the space for the healing to happen by being present with our hearts to love. Love is the unifying force of all creation." Who hasn't been burned by love? I thought of Jeremy and Miranda. I would hold the space for their healing.

With each subsequent week, I acquired more and more knowledge and skill. For instance, black stones are protective and grounding.

Jet is a calming, anti-hysteria stone.

Apache tear causes our ancestors to protect us.

Hemetite anchors energy and grounds it in the body.

Black tourmaline protects against psychic attack and electromagnetic pollution.

We learned that the aura has layers and each layer is a color, and that the chakras are located in the light body, which is pure energy and it feeds the physical vessel. Meridians carry the energy of the chakra into the body. Crystals get infused with our intent and affects the chakras.

We are each energy fields processing a multitude of different energies in order to manifest our physical being. Unwanted energies or intrusive entities can get stuck in our energy fields, causing imbalances in our energy centers that cause sickness, sadness, and loss of power.

Tauheedah taught us how to scan the client's energy using our palms. "The palms are portals, readers and transmitters. Our goal is to move stagnant energy out and to get the energy flowing. We are moving and shifting the energy in the light body."

She showed us how to lay crystals on the body, how to use different shamanic tools such as singing bowls, selenite, drums, rattles, bells, candles, oils, and feathers. Frankincense is a clearing oil and imparts beauty. "Put a couple of drops in your palm and swirl, fuse it with your own energy field. Use it with your hands hovering over the stones, or pre-treat the stones with it." Pure magic!

We each have our own gifts and style, there are no set rules, "use your intuition," she said. "And always call in your spirit guides to work with you, never work alone. These can be angels, ascended masters, ancestors, or guides."

So, the day came at The Imagine Center when I was ready to graduate—*if* I passed the exam. Each of us getting certified had to take a short written test and do a twenty-minute crystal healing in front of the class. Tauheedah would determine if we were certifiable. Okay... Adolfo, if you are reading this, please keep your mouth shut... thank-you!

Julie agreed to be my "client" and had just arrived. I kicked off my shoes, led her to the massage table, and asked her lie on her back. I closed my eyes and opened the space by calling in my angelic team and my guides. I gave thanks for their presence and the opportunity to assist Julie in her healing. I scanned her energy field with my hands, and then tested her chakras with my pendulum. Her third (solar plexus) and fourth (heart) chakras were blocked. *No hay problema*, I would get those suckers open and swirling in the right direction in no time.

I used my selenite wand and my breath to clear her energy field like a vacuum. Next I took crystals, onto which I'd add a drop of frankincense oil and held over a candle flame to bring up the healing properties, and placed them on and around her body one by one. I used rose quartz, green jade, and aventurine for her heart chakra, and citrine for her solar plexus. I placed a small piece of lapis on her throat, and I grounded her with magnetic hematite near her feet. I placed amethyst near her head to open psychic connection as well as helping to overcome fears and cravings. (I was still hoping she would give up the diet soda and also start eating more healthy foods.) I used clear quartz to amplify the other stones, and finally moonstone to enhance motivation. I shook a rattle around her body while pressing on the seams of her sides and legs to break up trapped and stagnant energy, and then cleared her with the selenite wand. I continued clearing with a large green turkey feather, and then sprayed some *palo santo* infused water in the air. I infused the crystals with my energy by sending light and love through my palms and then cleared her some more. Since this was a mini-session, and the twenty minutes were almost up, I began to remove the stones one by one with my intuition guiding me, and wrapped up the energy with my arms circling above my head, gave thanks to my guides and angels for the healing that had taken place. I gently assisted Julie off the table and gave her a glass of water and a piece of dark chocolate to ground her.

Tauheedah asked Julie to share her experience with the class.

"It was so relaxing. I could feel heat coming from Marla's palms, and energy shifting and moving. I also felt tingling in my palms. It was incredible," she beamed.

Tauheedah and the rest of the class clapped enthusiastically. "Beautiful! Beautiful!" said Tauheedah. "Marla, you are a powerful healer. Your specialty is getting the energy moving. It was just beautiful. Good job!"

Floating across the room, I escorted Julie out the door, and rejoined the class to watch the others do their healings.

We all passed the test. Tauheedah invited us to all sit down. She called each of us up individually and bestowed a blessing upon us and offered a message from our guides. Then she presented each of us with a certificate of completion and a gift of a piece of clear quartz in a silk pouch. I will treasure it always.

On my drive home, I contemplated the next step in becoming a healer. I would need to purchase a massage table. Tauheedah said that we could get a decent one on Amazon for a hundred bucks. I decided that I would sign up for a class to become attuned to Reiki immediately. Good thing I was in manifest mode, because this adventure would require some cold hard cash!

The Sad and Happy Ending

"Your soul belongs to the universe. Your mind is an outlet through which the Creative Intelligence of the universe seeks fulfillment."
~ Ernest Holmes

I was feeling extra sparkly since my crystal certification, but Julie's unhappy experience with her neighbor had prompted my own traumatic experiences. The little guy that runs the movie projector in my brain kept flashing images of my old boyfriend's face in flames, its blackened photo on the driveway. I heard again the revving sound of my car engine as it ground the remaining ashes to dust. I walked Macie through my neighborhood in the morning, reliving that crazy time of my life.

My boyfriend had kicked me in the shins, forcing me out of the house, and then slammed the door in my face. He was my lover, my roommate, and also my boss, so I not only had to find a new place to live, I also had to find a new job.

I don't know how I got myself into such a situation, but I do know that back in the 80s, *Drama* was my first name, followed by *Queen*.

Maybe I was being reminded of my own temporary insanity so I wouldn't judge my clients who did such dumb things. My poor client, Jeremy, had texted me that he was still seeing Miranda, the sugar-baby. Don't be a dumb schmuck, I wanted to tell him.

And then I thought of Fran. That's what Fran had told me. My dear Fran, a friend, yes, but so much more. I would be seeing her that afternoon in the hospital.

This surrogate Jewish momma had come into my life during those troubled times when I was a dumb schmuck. With my own mother a thousand miles away, it was nice to have an older, more experienced woman that I could talk to right there in the boyfriend's neighborhood. In a pinch, I could always get my mom on the phone, and she could reason with said boyfriend. Once, she assertively asked him to please *not* throw Marla's belongings in the street, and to calm down, because everything would be okay. That approach worked. For a while.

But when some ass-kickin' was in order, I called Fran, a hard-talkin', no bullshit-takin' lady. A svelte redhead (not natural; shhhh... our little secret) Fran had style and panache. Always dressed in a classy outfit, her hair and makeup were equally impeccable, and, man, did she know how to accessorize.

Fran was one of those women who never revealed her age and always thought she was right. A person had the right to two opinions, hers and hers—probably one of the reasons she never married. I met Fran when I was twenty years old and working as a hostess at a café in West Hollywood. She owned a teeny tiny little dress shop across the street called C'est Moi. Fran and I both loved all things French. Dress shop proprietor was just one of Fran's many careers. She'd also been a nightclub singer, a radio host, and a real estate investor.

"Marla, only a dumb schmuck would stay with this guy. You don't need to put up with that shit!" Fran said. "You are a beautiful young woman, and *he's* the real schmuck! You'll find someone else, *and* another job!" She was right, of course. Even though Fran had no qualms about using harsh language when needed, she was also deeply spiritual. We used to discuss the law of attraction and metaphysics. The teachings of spiritual philosophers such as Ernest Holmes, Thomas Troward, and Ralph Waldo Emerson were among our favorite topics of discussion. She would need those teachings more than ever now.

Sadly, Fran's age could no longer be hidden. That afternoon at Cedars-Sinai, I checked her medical chart, and there, for any visitor to see, was her date of birth.

Sitting on the edge of the bed, I gripped Fran's hand. Her penetrating brown eyes fixated on me.

"Do you know how old I am?" Her tone was less sassy, her volume weak.

I gave her a nod. *Yes, Fran, but go ahead and reveal your years.*

"Eighty!" Used to being independent and on the go, she spoke in a combination of disbelief and disgust.

Due to her loss of appetite, she'd withered away to a skeletal frame. I knew that she must have been mortified to be seen with no makeup and in this condition. Her red hair straggled from the knot tied on top of her head. She looked fragile and child-like, snuggled in her pink bed jacket and matching socks.

She'd had open-heart surgery three weeks prior. The doctors told her that it had been a success, but she wasn't recovering properly. She was in terrible pain and suffered from depression caused by the drugs and from being in bed for so long.

I'd been trekking back and forth from the valley to visit her every couple of days. Even if she wasn't awake or up for a visitor, I wanted her to know that someone was there for her.

"Listen, Marla, you have to help me," she said.

"What is it, Fran?"

"I want to die. I've had a good life." She looked down at herself and gestured with her hands. "This body is no good any more. Please help me die."

My eyes welled up with tears. "Oh, Fran, I'm so sorry you're uncomfortable and have to go through this. But the doctors say that there is nothing wrong with you now. You have no cancer, no disease. You just need to recover from the trauma of the heart surgery. It was a major ordeal, but it was a success. You *must* eat and get strong again."

Fran was defiant. "Eat the slop they serve here? Please Marla, I know you can do something. I want to die."

"Fran, even if I was willing to..." I stopped myself from saying *kill anyone, let alone a friend*. "...to do that, it's illegal. Do you want me to go to prison?"

"Adolfo! He's from Mexico. Doesn't he know someone?"

I looked at her as if she'd lost her mind, but she forged ahead.

"Maybe you could come into the place in a group, and then you can do it, and no one will know who did it...I wouldn't tell anyone! No one will know. You have to help me."

"Fran... Please...You know that isn't possible..."

"I want to die!"

My heart was breaking. She needed me and was miserable, but I couldn't do anything about it. "Fran, you will die, but not today... I cannot help you with this." I put my hand on her forehead. "Listen, Fran, meditate. You're connected to the Universe. Pray and ask God and the angels to help you. God will help you."

She nodded and closed her eyes.

My dear friend Peggy, the head Christian Chaplain at the hospital, appeared in the doorway. Peggy is an angel in human form and had been wonderful with Fran, visiting her every day, praying with her, and just being there as a loving presence. I got up and we went into the hallway. Fighting tears, I told her what Fran wanted.

"I know," Peggy said. "She's been saying that for the last couple of days. It's not unusual for patients to be depressed. We're sending in the psychiatrist to see her later to check her meds and see what we can do about her mood. She's lucky to have you, Marla."

"Well, I'm lucky to have her. Thirty years of friendship. She's very special to me."

"She loves you so much, like a daughter. She told me that she is leaving you a nest egg," said Peggy. "She wants you to be financially secure."

"I know, I was so honored when she told me that she put me in her will. She has been like a mother to me. But I can't believe she's ready to go. Although, she's so sure that her death would not be her end, so she's actually happy at the thought of shedding this life. It's the rest of us who will suffer. I don't know what I will do without Fran in my life. We didn't see each other very often, but she was always on the other end of the phone..."

"I'll come back later and give her some Reiki," said Peggy.

"That would be fantastic," I said. "Oh, and I want to tell you that I've been so inspired by the fact that the hospital—*Cedars-Sinai*—sent you to become a Reiki Master. With the amazing healing work that you've been doing, I've enrolled in a Reiki class myself, it starts next week."

Peggy took my hands in hers. "Marla, that's wonderful. Reiki is so powerful, it's amazing. It'll be a great addition to your crystal healing."

Yes...maybe I could. Seeing patients in the hospital suffering was gut-wrenching, and I kept feeling I could help. Peggy's words resonated with me. With the use of crystals *and* Reiki, maybe I could become a healer. I'd always wanted to be an entertainer or a writer as a child, but I'd become so connected to the spirit world. I love the idea of evolving so that my work matches my spiritual energy. In my perfect life, I'd be both a writer and a healer. Ironically, the very people who needed my healing were my clients. Would it be possible to shift the energy of the men who demanded perfection? Maybe I could heal their pain and get to the heart of what they truly longed for. Could it really be possible? Maybe the matchmaking industry was where I was meant to stay...

I fought the LA traffic and finally made it home after an hour and a half—just to go fifteen frickin' miles. I needed to unwind. Julie and I planned to go to candlelight yoga that night. We loved the little yoga studio that was tucked in the back of a strip mall in Encino. Eva, the owner who also teaches, was one of those women who exudes spirituality. Her zen-like energy kept us coming back for more.

At 7:30 that evening, Romeo made sure Julie knew I had arrived. He has a great vocal range for such a little guy. Excited to show me her newly acquired antique apothecary chest, Julie led me into her bedroom. She mimicked Vanna White as she posed in front of the dark wood chest with thirty little drawers.

"For all of my herbs...I have sixty different kinds now," she said, beaming.

I must have looked confused.

"You know, for my Candle Magick!"

"Oh...my gosh, Julie, this is amazing! You're really serious about this."

She opened a larger drawer on the bottom and pulled out a beautiful blue candle (signifying calmness, protection, and wisdom) adorned with glitter and herbs.

"Here you go. I thought this might help with what you are going through with Fran. I infused it with peaceful intentions, so it should make your mediation more powerful."

It had been a teary day and the waterworks started up again. "Julie, this is so sweet. You are amazing. Thank you." I threw my arms around her in gratitude, and Romeo jumped up on the bed, baring his teeth at me.

Julie quickly scolded him. "Romeo! This is NOT how you behave to guests. Really. I am so ashamed."

I approached Romeo as his scowl became more menacing.

I calmly assured him, "Romeo, darling, I WILL win you over one day. You shall see."

We pulled up to the yoga studio fifteen minutes early, but the door was still locked. Eva was probably stuck in traffic. There was a massage place next door, and shades covered its window and the glass door as well, yet we could see posters of feet with the reflexology points.

I suggested we check it out. We both love massages and often indulged in bargain Chinese massages at places that offered a sixty-minute combo—a full-body massage and foot reflexology, all for twenty bucks. The treatments are given in places that seemed to be popping up on every corner in the San Fernando Valley with dimly lit warehouse-like rooms lined with rows of La-Z-Boy-style recliners and no bamboo screens or trickling fountains in sight. The massages are strictly choreographed with no deviation from the routine, so it's a crapshoot when trying a new spot. I like my massages deep. Put some elbow grease into it, would you?

The lighting inside this new spot was dim, but that was typical, yet no one waited at the front counter. I could see many cubicles lining a short hallway. The list of services posted on the wall seemed pretty standard.

Swedish massage 55.00

Deep tissue/acupressure 60 minutes: 50.00

Reflexology: 35.00 ½ hour

Hot stone massage: 75.00 90 minutes

Aromatic oil massage: 60 minutes 75.00

A petite Chinese woman silently appeared and pulled a curtain closed behind her.

"Oh, hello," Julie said. "We just stopped in to check the place out. We're taking a yoga class next door in a few minutes."

The woman stared at us with a frozen smile.

"I see that you do aromatic oil massage," I said, pointing to the menu.

A glazed look in her eyes, the woman emitted a garbled *yahhah*.

"Do *you* do the oil massage?" I asked.

"Ahhh ..." Blank stare and semi smile.

"Do you speak English?" asked Julie.

"Ah... no..." She nodded *yes* like a zombie.

Julie and I looked at each other, dumbfounded. How on earth could this woman not know simple English and run a business.

"Soooo ... If we want to come in, do we need an appointment?" I asked.

Zombie deer frozen in the headlights.

"Okay, well, never mind..." said Julie. "Thanks anyway."

We let ourselves out feeling like we'd just exited The Twilight Zone. Eva arrived and unlocked the door, and a few students trickled into the studio. We paid our sixteen dollars, took off our shoes, and stored them with our bags in the wall cubbies.

"Eva, the strangest thing just happened next door." I explained the odd encounter with the Chinese woman.

Eva pulled us aside and in a hushed voice said, "That woman doesn't actually want *your* business...if you catch my drift..."

"Ohhhhhhh!!!! Their massages lead to happy endings?" I squealed.

Eva nodded. "You should see the Ferraris and Lamborghinis pulling up here for quick nooners!"

Julie was aghast. "RIGHT HERE IN ENCINO?"

"And afterwards the men notice the pretty women coming to yoga class and come in for a chat."

"Just out of curiosity," I asked, "what do they charge?"

"Oh, it can range from 1,200 to 3,000 bucks. The place gets raided about once a month. The police come, take all of their cash, close them down, but they're back in business the next day."

That's because what the clientele paid for wasn't a happy *ending* at all, but a quickly fading pleasure that demanded repetition. To most of us, death is an ending, but Fran would call it a happy beginning of the next phase. We agreed that much of what we think is going to provide a happy ending never really does because there are no endings.

As Eva guided us through gentle stretches, I contemplated the last thirty years. In my twenties, I jumped in and out of relationships, looking for a happy ending to my loneliness, even getting married on a whim. Yet, my husband was unfaithful, and we struggled to make ends meet. My thirties were spent searching for myself after the whim ended in divorce, a most unhappy one. My grief carried me to Chicago where I learned self-reliance, a happy outcome, but not an ending. In LA, I met Adolfo, a beginning, and started gaining some traction throughout my forties, establishing a career for myself and going for my dreams. Entering my fifth decade here on earth, I was surrendering to a higher purpose that came fluttering out from my heart like a monarch butterfly, perfect in its beauty, finally released from its cocoon.

Eva led us in a short meditation to make us feel balanced and centered, and I did. I felt like I glittered with fairy dust, at one with the Universe, ready to fly into a life of harmony and service. Then, as the session ended—happily—I thought of coming home to Adolfo. He was already a nervous wreck about the fact that I was taking such an interest in this whole healing/angel/crystal/ spiritual/occult world. If I dared to totally switch directions in life, from Cupid to Healer, I needed to tread delicately and stealthily so as not to alarm him any further. I hated to keep secrets from my beloved, but this was about self-preservation in the sense of preserving my truest self and therefore saving my soul.

As Julie and I left the studio, she said, "Well, looks like you sure had a happy ending!"

I grinned. "Way happier than the dudes next door. And longer lasting. I feel fantastic. You?"

"Totally. And *virtuous*." She snickered at the massage parlor. "Schmucks."

Driving home, I kept thinking of the men paying thousands of dollars for sex and how men also paid me thousands of dollars to find their dream woman. I wanted to see myself on a mission to match soul mates, but was I really just a variation of that old Chinese madam? Was I on a path to end up like her? Just thinking about my clients specifying trivial qualities for their life partners threatened to hose down my fairy-dust feeling.

Could I earn my way while staying on a spiritual high? Chop wood, carry water. I got that. Noble and honorable. No problem. But I also wanted more, something that contributed to a higher consciousness throughout the planet. I wanted to help others feel as good as I felt in that moment—and, well, get paid for it.

It's Dad! It's Dad!

"Be not too hasty to trust or admire the teachers of morality; they discourse like angels but they live like men."
~ Samuel Johnson, lexicographer (18 Sep 1709-1784)

Just before retiring on the night of the massage, I made myself an herbal tea, and then settled into bed with a book called, *Essential Reiki, A Complete Guide To An Ancient Healing Art.* I figured I would get a head start on the new modality I would be learning. I hadn't told Adolfo yet that I would be attending a weekend Reiki certification class and was avoiding that conversation as long as possible.

I so often felt sad that I couldn't share my hopes, dreams, plans, goals, insights, or interests with Adolfo since he would inevitably shoot them down. Other than my business, virtually everything I became interested in, earned a lecture from him. I was not thinking about priorities, not thinking from a standpoint of reality, or I was just plain crazy. I had better stick to matchmaking because that was where I made money. "You should be grateful!" he would say about my career.

I know that makes him sound mean-spirited, and his attitude often sent me on long, tearful walks with Macie. Adolfo wanted me to be happy; I didn't doubt that, but he insisted on being the Captain of the mothership. No rocking the boat allowed and no co-captains. Though he sometimes caused me great pain and anguish, I did realize where his negativity was coming from.

Adolfo grew up in an affluent, old Mexican family whose roots went all the way back to the conquistadores in Spain. Certain streets bore the names of his forbearers in many towns in Mexico. He grew up with maids, nannies, chauffeurs, and bodyguards, scurrying to serve the family. Unfortunately, bad investments, a change in government, and other disasters depleted the family's wealth. His parents became elderly and in need of help. For many years, Adolfo supported them and his younger brother, sending a large portion of his income to Mexico monthly. After his parents passed away, and his younger brother married, Adolfo could finally allocate his hard-earned money toward buying *our* own home and planning for *our* future. I know that in his mind, he was making up for lost time, and if we weren't careful, we could end up like his parents, out of cash and in desperate need of our children's assistance. Only, we had no children, and unfortunately, Macie did not have a job.

Not that she wasn't clever enough to be in the movies— which I did consider for a nanosecond or two. I'd taught her a dozen tricks, and I could see her landing a role like that Jack Russell terrier cast as "Eddie" on the TV show Frasier. Becoming a talent manager, even for a dog, was like any other actor's merry-go-round, of course, and it wouldn't exactly be the high-minded direction I longed for.

I read a few chapters of the Reiki book, but was soon asleep when Adolfo came in from work around midnight. He switched on the Tiffany style lamp on the nightstand. I pulled my sleep mask up off of my eyes and listened to him chatter about his night as he undressed. It always takes him about an hour to unwind after a night of performing and schmoozing. He turned on the TV to an episode of one of our favorite shows, "American Greed." Still half asleep, I heard Stacy Keach's commanding voice announce, "Kevin Trudeau's Secrets." I immediately perked up. Kevin was a former client. What was he doing on this scandal show? The truth spilled out.

Infomercial kingpin Kevin Trudeau makes millions selling baldness cures, weight loss programs, and get rich schemes on late night television. But when the FTC cries foul, fining him $37.6 million, Trudeau pulls his most brazen scam yet—claiming he's completely broke.

Before I had my own business, I worked for a Beverly Hills service that catered to a wealthy clientele, let's just call it "Double D Dating." I'd first started working as a matchmaker there well over a decade ago, and Kevin was one of the clients. A minor celebrity was still a celebrity, and I was so excited to be matching him. I had actually taken his mega memory course when I lived in Chicago in the 90's, so I knew who he was. I still use some of the practices. Kevin went on to write books on health and weight loss and even did an audio course on the law of attraction that I thought was fantastic. Granted, he was a shameless pitchman, and made millions of dollars hawking his wares on infomercials, and at seminars, always making amazing claims. Yet he didn't *steal* from people. He *sold* his products—granted by employing the "greater fool" theory, making something dubious seem like a bargain because there were greater fools out there who would pay "twice the price." Of course, he didn't call them that. Most of the cases highlighted on the program "American Greed" were men who had done Ponzi schemes, or swindled unsuspecting people out of their life savings. Those guys deserved to rot in jail, but I was a bit surprised to see Kevin highlighted on the show. Still, he no doubt hired the best lawyers, and despite that, a jury of his peers found him guilty of fraud.

I remember chatting with Kevin on the phone when my first book was published. We were talking about writing, and he claimed that he wrote his books basically in one shot, just dictated them with no editing whatsoever. And these were books that were hundreds of pages long, books that needed a lot of research. I knew that had to be bullshit, but hey, I admired his go-get-'em attitude, and I thought that at least some of his books contained useful information. No one is all bad, and there were many positive sides to Kevin.

I remembered how he claimed the government was out to get him, and he accused its agencies of conspiring to suppress low costs and common remedies, including those for cancer. Of the medical-pharmaceutical complex, Kevin often asked if you had a business that made you well over a hundred billion dollars per year, would you take steps to eradicate the need for your business or would you make every effort to keep that money continue rolling in? His logic was compelling, although in Kevin's case, he may have been projecting his own greed onto others. I certainly know of many dedicated doctors who get infuriated with this type of accusation. And yet, Western medicine steadfastly ignores the horrendous flood of new toxins out there, so we turn to alternatives, making us vulnerable to hucksters like Kevin.

Many people in the alternative health industry and people into natural healing feel that it's up to them to bridge this gap. Self-healed yoga priestess Christina Sarich writes that our blood and bones now contain over 85,000 different chemical pollutants, including depleted uranium from bombs and nuclear energy sites like Fukushima. Toxic mold and chemicals as sinister as Agent Orange are now part of our genetic makeup, not to mention our daily dose of pesticides, preservatives, GMOs, hormones, additives in our food and water, and pollutants in the air. Sarich says all these toxins have seeped into our cells, causing cancer, depression, and even insanity. Our hormonal systems are so out of whack that both boys and girls are starting puberty way too soon, and fetuses are not developing properly. ADHD, ADD, and autism are on the rise like never before. Our bodies are fat and tired too, because a toxic body has to work so hard to process the contaminants, it can't metabolize fats and proteins properly. Yes, Kevin Trudeau exploited people's fears, but he was not entirely wrong.

Many years ago, I also played Cupid for another celebrated spiritual guru, who was charismatic, well spoken, and successful with loads of followers. I was excited at the prospect of finding him his soul mate, but I was surprised to learn that, as spiritually evolved as he seemed to be, when it came to women, he was, in fact, a mere man like all of the rest of my clients. He insisted on finding a super skinny *ten* to spend his life with, and if she wasn't brunette, well, forget it. And then the unthinkable happened. Like Kevin, he ended up in prison. He was found guilty of negligent homicide when things went wrong at a spiritual retreat in the desert.

Spiritual leaders are important and can help us get to where we want to go, but I always remind myself to take everyone's advice with a serving of skepticism. After all, these people did not arrive on a silver cloud descended from the heavens. They are mere mortals just like the rest of us. And part of the enlightenment process involves each individual deciding for themselves what is most true. There are so many seeds and kernels of truth in the vast amounts of loam out there, flecks of gold in the rocky ores. I am the harvester, the miner. I sift and pan, growing more discerning, building spiritual muscles as I mull over the vast mysteries, and my spirit makes its peace with the universe.

I closed my eyes that night, and Adolfo turned off the TV, but a few minutes later, I found myself standing next to the bed, looking up into the corner of the bedroom, in awe of what I saw coming towards me. A bright light seemed to have opened up, shining outwards, and out of that light, someone was coming! It scared me at first, as I had never seen a bright light coming out of nowhere like that before. I mean, I sensed that something/someone was coming from another dimension but who/what? I willed myself to stand firm and keep looking into the light even though I was scared out of my wits. Then a thrill came over me like I had never felt in my life. My father, who had died over a decade ago, was entering my room.

I shouted, "IT'S DAD! IT'S DAD!" I couldn't see him, but I *knew* it was him. "IT'S DAD!"

All of a sudden, I was back in my bed, sitting up, and my dad had settled at the end of my bed. I quickly scrambled over to him and put my hand on his arm. He was wearing a brown hooded cloak, like a monk. His face looked thinner than I remembered. I blurted out the words as fast as I could, "I love you, I love you, I love you, I love you."

We stared deeply into each other's eyes and he nodded slightly letting me know that yes, it was really dad, and that everything was okay. And then he was gone.

Why hadn't he stayed longer? I crawled back under the covers. Adolfo was asleep. I turned on my side, back to him, in complete awe of what had just transpired and tried to make sense of how this could have happened without Adolfo hearing me yell. The logical explanation was that I was somehow dreaming, but I'd never had any dream like this in my life. Dreams morph and twist into other dreams, some more powerful than others. They are fleeting and hard to pin down. This experience was nothing like that. It felt strange, but real. Even stranger was that monk's cloak. In life, Dad had insisted he was an atheist. And he was certainly not interested in anything approaching a monastic life of contemplation and prayer, of denial of earthly pleasures. He lived like a man, bad habits and all and made no pretenses to anything different. He was a good man, though, and he loved me. That look in his eyes...he wanted me to understand something. Maybe the monk's hood was a way of showing without speaking that his spirit had entered a different phase and that it was evolving into a more advanced consciousness. I slept then, deeply, peacefully, and long.

In the morning, Macie and I took a long leisurely stroll. The light seemed especially dazzling, sparkling. The leaves were more vibrant, the squirrels and I were one, and I felt even more connected to the Universe than I had at my yoga session. I tuned into my spirit, my higher self for answers. The only explanation that I could conceive of was that I had astral traveled. I had met my dad on the astral plane.

Getting My Buzz On

"If you want to find the secrets of the universe, think in terms of energy, frequency and vibration." ~ Nikola Tesla

Two weeks after I met my dad on the astral plane, Fran left her body. I placed a candle and a framed black and white glossy photo of Fran in her younger days when she was a gorgeous model on the antique desk that once belonged to Fran's mother. Fran had not only left me a little nest egg in the way of cash, but also gifted me her beloved desk. I would cherish it always. I also made the decision to put Fran's money into my retirement account. Every penny. A girlfriend tried to convince me to buy a Mini Cooper once I got the money. I have always dreamed of buying a new Mini in Hunter Green, but Fran worked hard for her money, and I would honor her by not squandering it. My eight-year-old Toyota Scion would last me another few years at least.

I like to think that my dad and Fran were hanging out together in the astral suburbs, planning another visit one day soon. It was a lovely sentiment. That unchained optimism that I told you about was coming in pretty handy. I just knew that the Universe was self-organizing and flowing in a dance of absolute perfection. Yes, we all have challenges and heartbreaks, but everything would turn out in the end. After all, energy cannot be destroyed. Bashar, an extraterrestrial channeled through Darryl Anka, says that if we exist, we will always exist, and that if we are in physical form on earth, *"there is just a sliver of ourselves in the body. Our Higher Self is the spirit part of us that 'resides' in the nonphysical realm. It's our Divine spark."* I believe that this part of us helps us to keep on track with our life's purpose and in touch with our "highest excitement" as Bashar would say. So, the sliver of the soul in Fran and dad's physical bodies slid back into Source, back to the non-physical realm, never to be destroyed, morphing into other experiences of themselves. They are now residing in another frequency. We are flipping through other frequencies like a radio. Let's say we are tuned into 97.1 FM and enjoying the music on that station. That does not mean that is the only station out there broadcasting. There are hundreds of other stations emitting frequencies simultaneously that people can tune into just by changing the channel. Could it be that meeting my dad on the astral plane was possible because both of us tuned into each other's frequency and met in the middle?

Since I had been delving into new modalities and study, the word *energy* has taken on a whole new meaning. Everything in creation is made up of electromagnetic energy, vibrating at different frequencies that correspond to sound, light, and color. The existence of electromagnetic fields around every object in the world is a scientifically proven fact. Psychics might see them as auras. The Chinese refer to this energy as *chi*, the vital life-force energy of the Universe, present within every living thing. Ancient Egyptians had a similar concept, *ankh*.

There was no doubt in my mind that this was real, because I often felt surges of energy, as if the *chi* was doing the cha-cha-cha up and down my meridians. My hands would heat up and tingle out of the blue as if to say, *Okay, Marla, let's get healing! Find someone to work on.* I loved the feel of energy coursing through me steadily ever since I received the attunements in my weekend training from my Reiki master, Katt Lowe.

My initial encounter with this *Reiki buzz* was on the first day of class. Katt taught me, along with nine other students, about the history and use of Reiki and then shared fascinating stories of her experiences with Reiki. She had astonished her doctors by healing herself of giant fibroid tumors. The class would partner up and take turns placing our hands above our partner's hands and feeling the energy, amazed at the tingle almost as if it were humming or buzzing. We also stood behind our seated partners and placed our hands first on their shoulders—hands-on Reiki—and then hovering just above their shoulders—hands-off Reiki. Each of us then gave our account of what we felt, if anything. Both my partner and I noticed that our hands started "buzzing" and continued throughout the class.

This mysterious power can reveal itself in unusual ways. I had recently asked Adolfo to help me with my computer; it seemed to have frozen, and I was at a loss. Adolfo was sitting at his desk in his studio, my Macbook Pro in his lap. I stood behind him, peering over his shoulder, trying to learn what to do if it should happen again. The first clue of his frustration with my uncooperative computer was the expletives he spewed as he addressed my laptop. I intuitively raised my hands over his head and started letting Reiki flow from my hands, hoping it would calm him down. A few minutes later, my computer was unstuck, and I went out to the kitchen and started scrubbing some veggies for my daily glass of "green gunk."

Adolfo shot out of his studio, screaming like a banshee, "what in the hell did you do to me?"

I dropped my kale in the sink and spun around to face him. "What are you talking about?"

"I almost had a stroke! What did you do?"

What could I have done? Accidentally hit a dangerous button on his sound system? Slobber on his chair? "Ummmm..." The Reiki? "Well, I did direct some Reiki energy to help calm you down."

A look of horror distorted his features. "Never do that again! That is dangerous. Just because you took a class and got a certificate, you think you know what you are doing? It takes years of study to be able to do Reiki!"

"Adolfo, that is not true. Anyone can do Reiki once attuned. Reiki does no harm, it is just energy, it is not possible to do harm."

"Well, I feel dizzy and nauseous. Are you trying to kill me? You're dangerous. Never do that to me again!"

Adolfo went back into his studio, and I hustled into my office and emailed Katt. I explained what had occurred and Adolfo's claims. Katt responded immediately and assured me that, of course, Reiki couldn't do any harm. "But sometimes someone can have a 'healing crisis,' and toxins are released, possibly causing a little nausea. That's the only explanation I can think of." So, if I'd given him a glass of water, he probably would have been fine.

My darling Adolfo was set on fighting me as if I'd brought toxic germs into the house. I rarely let myself be intimidated any longer, though. I knew that I was on the right path, and that was all that mattered. He would come around, eventually. Once I'd been doing this long enough, and he saw that people were benefitting from my healing treatments, he would come to understand how important this work was to me.

As if anticipating Julie's call a few days later, my hands were "buzzing" when she called to complain about her stressful day. Not only did one of her clients bounce a check on a payment that had already been three months late, it seemed that her crush, Sergio, had a new girlfriend, and Julie found it nearly impossible to stop herself from peering out her window from behind her curtains, noting their comings and goings.

"She's blonde. And attractive. And drives a Mercedes," she moaned over the phone.

"My hands are buzzing," I said, "Get your butt over here, and I'll do an energy clearing and some Reiki." Julie loved our Reiki sessions and arrived a few minutes later as I was clearing the area with sage. I didn't even get a chance to set up the table.

We passed through the kitchen before going into my sanctuary.

"Something to drink? Diet coke?" I knew that an offer of "green gunk" would be rebuffed.

"Thanks, but no. Actually, I'll have a glass of water."

I must have looked like I was having a stroke, so she quickly explained.

"I know you're in shock. Hey, I might be a mess over Sergio, but I *am* trying to make some better choices health-wise. I've joined a place that teaches Dahn Yoga. It's right near my house. I pay $150.00 per month and can go as much as I want, so I've been going every night for the past two weeks."

"Julie, that is fantastic! What is Dahn Yoga? I have never heard of it."

"Well, to be honest, I'm not exactly sure myself, but I'm having fun. The people are really nice, and I feel that it is helping me get on track with my attitude towards taking better care of myself. I do know that it's a Korean system of yoga that puts emphasis on emotional, physical and spiritual well-being. It combines tai chi, yoga, and martial arts exercises. And, well, it's supposed to help us to become a lot more happy, healthy, and peaceful. You should come with me one night. I really think you'd like it, especially Friday nights. We dance!"

Once in my sanctorum, I began working on Julie while she was standing. I checked her chakras and cleared them, and then she sat on my new purple crushed velvet chair, bought on sale at Pier One Imports. I performed a Reiki treatment, starting on her shoulders.

"This feels amazing Marla, my hands and lips are buzzing," said Julie.

I loved hearing the affirmation that Julie could feel the energy. I knew she needed empowerment and mentally pictured the Reiki power symbol as I moved my hands to Julie's head.

I was attuned by Katt into Reiki I and II. In traditional Reiki there are three Reiki symbols given during the Reiki II Attunement (initiation). They are: the power symbol (Choku Rei), the mental/emotional symbol (Sei He Ki), and the Distance symbol (Hon Sha Ze Sho Nen). Many Reiki Masters consider the Reiki symbols holy and persist in the old Reiki tradition that they must be kept secret. When a Reiki practitioner draws, thinks about, or visualizes a symbol, it will instantly connect to the energies it represents.

Katt's words popped into my head. *Giving Reiki will never deplete you, because you are not using your own energy, it is Universal energy flowing through you. Whenever you give a healing, you get a healing.*

When I completed the session, I handed Julie her water. "Be sure to drink plenty of filtered water after a session. Energy is shifting throughout your body, re-balancing, and triggering the cleansing process, so water will help flush toxins from your body, plus help to conduct your body's energy flow," I explained.

Julie moved from the velvet chair to my love seat and Macie jumped into her lap. "So have you taken any new classes lately?"

"There are some that I am looking into. That reminds me, I almost forgot to tell you. It's about a controversial new class I was invited to take that is gaining popularity in Los Angeles."

"Really? Do tell..."

"I went to a woman's networking group a couple of weeks ago..." I told her how it was held in a beautiful home in Westwood. There was a guest speaker, who spoke about astrology, but before that, wine was served and a nice buffet, so we could eat and mingle. I took my plate and found a spot in the living room on a large ottoman. An attractive gal of about thirty-five came and sat down next to me on the ottoman. We exchanged pleasantries and talked about how delicious the vegan couscous was. She handed me a five by seven glossy card with her info on it and said that she was an orgasmic meditation teacher. "'I'd like to offer you a free class,' she said in this professional voice like she was offering a class in estate planning."

Julie stopped patting Macie. "What in the heck is orgasmic meditation?"

"Well, I am not exactly sure, but the woman said that she had extensive training and that it's very freeing and powerful. It's supposed to be therapeutic, rather than sexual. But then she said, 'if nothing else, it's nice to just go get your clit stroked for fifteen minutes.'"

"WHAAAAT? MARLA! YOU ARE NOT SERIOUS!"

Macie jumped off the couch and under my chair for protection.

"I know. I just about spewed my couscous. I told her that I needed to refill my chardonnay and skedaddled."

"But, Marla, I don't understand. What *is* it?"

"Right. So, I looked it up when I got home. You are NOT going to believe this is going on! They actually call it *OM*, short for *Orgasmic Meditation*. It's the practice of stimulation of the upper-left quadrant of the clitoris by a fully-clothed partner, usually male, though not always. You lie down, nude from the waist down on your back on a yoga matt in a "nest," made up of pillows and blankets, legs splayed open like a frog."

"No... no, nonono ..."

"Yep, and get this...The fully dressed stroker, before he begins any touch, describes his partner's soon-to-be-stroked vagina in detail."

Julie's arm shot up in the air, palm out, as if stopping a runaway train. "HOLD IT... WHAAAA... WHAT???"

"Yeah... well, there's more..."

Julie gulped her water. Even Macie was giving me a funny look. "Go on."

"Well, apparently, the guy sets a timer for fifteen minutes, asks permission to touch her, touching her legs with his hands, and then gets his finger in place under the hood of her clit. He then applies a small amount of lubricant, oh, and he is wearing gloves, mind you, so this is all very sanitary and clinical, and he uses a very slight, small, up-down stroking motion, and the woman is supposed to notice her own sensations."

"As opposed to ignoring them?"

"Er...well, yeah, I guess. I mean, a client shouldn't just enjoy herself, or else what would she need the 'expert' for?"

Julie kept shaking her head. "And this is done in a room with other people?"

"Yeah. Creepy, huh. Personally, I would rather get beaten with bamboo."

"And, like, higher frequencies and cosmic energy and vibrations, and all that...but what's wrong with a good old-fashioned vibrator?"

I laughed. "Well, I guess each to her own."

"Can you imagine a class like this for guys?" Julie looks comically orgasmic. "Left side? Right side...? Ohh, golly! Woo-hoo! Thank you, Jesus!"

Such a moment on top of a great Reiki session...we laughed ourselves silly, so light-hearted, we almost levitated right then and there.

A Collective of Twelve

"I think immortality is the passing of a soul through many lives or experiences, and such as are truly lived, used and learned, help on to the next, each growing richer, happier and higher, carrying with it only the real memories of what has gone before."
~ Louisa May Alcott

Certain channelers have fascinated me for years, and I've spent countless hours on YouTube watching incredible sessions with these people. Time and again they say astonishing things that feel not only true, but as if I'd always known these concepts, deep down. Addressing any number of wild questions from their audiences, they spew brilliant explanations without hesitation. Yale-educated with a master's degree, medium Paul Selig says of the material he channels that he can't quite believe it, yet he "knows" it. Esther Hicks, who channels Abraham, is one of my favorites, and I also love listening to an entity that medium Darryl Anka says is an eternal self, based in another world, referred to as *Bashar*. Bashar's no-nonsense approach of patience and wry, spontaneous humor makes listeners squirm, think, nod in moments of discovery, and laugh. Of course, two of the most famous channelers of our time were Jane Roberts, who channeled Seth, and Edgar Cayce, a medical intuitive as well as a channeler who reintroduced us to Atlantis and Lemuria.

My Reiki master, Katt told me about Grace Cavanaugh, who is a channel for a collective of twelve called *Osairah*. She also channels other masters, high beings of light, as well as Mother Mary, often described by other channelers as infinitely loving and available to help the humans of our planet.

Katt said that Grace was the real deal. Since I trusted Katt, I had called and made an appointment for a private session. Wouldn't it be amazingly wonderful if Mother Mary came through in my session that day, I thought? I know Mother Mary, love her, and have offered many prayers to her, but this *Osairah*? I had only a small idea of what to expect from talking to Katt and from the website.

Osairah is described as a family of light, which means that there are thousands of them. They are a collective group for higher consciousness, souls and beings, many of whom have incarnated and many who haven't. At any given time as Grace is preparing to channel, twelve of them feel the call and come. I can't help but imagine little cosmic negotiations.

So, Omicron, can you take my Earth-human shift for me? I covered for you last week.

Okay, Orpheus, but can you stall while I finish my celestial energy bar?

Actually, as I understand it, they may have distinct qualities, but their personalities don't need names. Grace says that she feels as if she's in a deep meditation as her ego self "moves aside," and they enter her and converge as one voice to speak.

I approached her modest single-family ranch-style home—a bit of a disconnect because a temple would seem more appropriate for such lofty spirits. Grace and two enthusiastic medium-sized dogs greeted me at the door and escorted me into the living room.

"Make yourself comfortable," she said, motioning toward the cushy sofa. A beautiful forty-something blonde, Grace could easily fit into my database of what many of my male clients where seeking physically, although... I could just see her sitting across from a date at a posh restaurant in a get-acquainted conversation.

> *Mark: So Grace, Marla mentioned that you're in the spiritual development field. What does that mean?*
>
> *Grace: (pausing as she nibbles organic green salad) I'm a trance channel for a collective of twelve entities from the 5th, 7th 9th and 11th dimensions called Osairah.*
>
> *Mark: (deer-in-headlights expression followed by a frozen smile, head bobbing like a dashboard doll) Okay... wow... I see...*

Grace was in a relationship though, so, this was a moot issue. Her "foster" dogs, rescued from a shelter, jumped up onto my lap and showered me with kisses. Grace ushered them into the back yard, returned, lit a couple of candles, and sat across from me in a comfy armchair. She has a personality that made me feel at ease right away. Her face has an etheric glow, and her smile is warm. She has experienced metaphysical "miracles" that I can still only dream of. I mean, *Mother Mary?* I felt like I was in kindergarten in the presence of a Harvard graduate.

Grace explained that Osairah would come in and give me a greeting and a message and then I was free to ask my questions. The session would be recorded, so no need to take notes. My excitement surged, and I felt giddy. Grace closed her eyes and took several long deep breaths. And then...

Hmmmm... Indeed, greetings to you, dear one. We are that one known as O-sai-rah. In fact, we are overjoyed in this moment for all the excitement we are recognizing. We say to you that life in your third dimensional reality is not always the smooth line you'd like it to be. Ha!

We are overjoyed at this moment in this timeline to be present. We are recognizing you on many frequencies—dimensions—and we are connected very strongly. We are the ones known as O-sai-rah, the collective of twelve this day in par-ti-cu-lar, connected to you from what you would understand to be seventh dimensional energies, fifth dimensional energies, eleventh dimensional energies and ninth dimensional energies. We say to you that we are all participating from those dimensions that you are also aligned with, dear one, the multi-dimensional self that you are.

Many lifetimes you have had, dear one, not only on this planet. Many thousands of lifetimes you have had. There is a frequency code color; we are recognizing it as a very beautiful aquamarine color. You have extraordinary blue ray energy as well. You have seventh dimensional energy, and you have not come here by accident. There are no accidents. It is as if you have melded many of the frequencies of the previous lifetimes.

It is no accident that we are sitting with you here today, we come from what you would call and consider the future of your life and lifetimes and what you would consider our past, so we are merging on your third dimensional reality in this way because there is the access point, there is the convergence.

We can say to you that this purposeful meeting is aligned. We can assure you that you are perfectly on time, and we say to you, dear one, it is good to see you again, dear friend, because we recognize you and what you would say from previous time lines, many dimensions, and what you would say, past lives.

We are recognizing in some ways what you would understand the word to be ancientness in you, dear one. You have a very strong alignment and you have lived many lifetimes in what is known as Lemuria. This is a frequency home for you.

You have many lifetimes as a very wise being. We see you as a very strong tall masculine man, where we recognize to be Peru, having a very strong understanding of the stars and numbers. This was a carryover from Lemuria. You were considered to be a very wise being [in Peru], 2,000 years before the 2,000-year timeline.

I didn't relate to the Peruvian identity, but I'd always wanted to go to Machu Pichu, now even more so. I'd heard of Lemuria and was fascinated about this ancient civilization which reportedly existed prior to and during the time of Atlantis. It is believed that Lemuria may have been located in the Southern Pacific Ocean, and there actually are sunken continents in the area, visible from satellite mapping. One of them is referred to as "Zealandia" because New Zealand was part of it. At its peak of civilization, the Lemurian people were said to be both highly evolved and very spiritual. Osairah continued:

> We are recognizing your spirit self, your soul, your essence. Much of your intent comes from seventh dimensional energy, what we understand to be the angelic dimension.
>
> You have much soul family in the seventh dimension. Your seventh dimensional connection is the family of light that you know there.
>
> You also have ninth dimensional energy very strongly aligned with you as well. That alignment is very strongly Pleiadian. The connection to that is a very interesting timeline that you would consider a future timeline.

The Pleiades as a point of extra-terrestrial connection and possibly even origins is a common idea among many in the New Age community. Pleiadians come from the Pleiades, a star cluster in the constellation of Taurus. Although the Pleiadians are 541 light years away, they are said to be able to navigate the cosmos to other worlds. Channelers and psychics attuned to the notion say the Pleiadians are coming now, sometimes in physical form but most often through human consciousness, to help us evolve.

Osairah continued to talk about my frequencies, and then they opened up to my questions.

"Osairah, what do you see me doing in the future? Will I still be matchmaking? I have so many interests, there doesn't seem to be enough time in the day to pursue everything."

What we want to tell our human friends is that you are the best guide, but we can give you pointers. The path is more lit up this way.

When we recognize your frequency, we see you have followed the bread crumbs—haha, very good—meaning diligently you have listened within, and you followed your heart's desires in certain ways, codes, and frequencies, often to the dismay of others, the idea that you would veer and go in different directions.

You have literally been a captain of a sea vessel, we see three lifetimes, very strongly a propensity towards the sea, one was also a treasure hunter, even in this lifetime, an aspect of what it is within you which is to adventure, to know more, to see more, to grasp life's deeper meanings and messages. Your joy is the most important thing for you to follow.

This fascinated me. It was true that I have listened within and followed my heart's desires, *often to the dismay of others*. I was bullied in school as a child, carrying anger toward my persecutors. Yet looking back, I see that the behavior of certain kids was possibly a reaction to witnessing my enthusiasm. Maybe my unrestricted magic and light that emanated from my soul touched a painful blister in those who couldn't access their own magic and light. I do believe that all of us come from pure source energy, but not all of us recognize that in ourselves and therefore can easily lash out at others blessed with such carefree expression.

My dear friend Rouben, who is like a father to me, sees my pursuit of my many interests and often tells me, "Marla, you are turning every stone, you don't give up, and one day you will hit it big time." Osairah underscored this direction.

You came here for your soul's intentional purpose to expand, to know itself, to be the light of the crystal that you are. Remember that you are a beingness of eternal light, you are a beingness of God consciousness. You are innocence, an angel on this planet, embodying a physical body that you have come forth to be the fullness of that. Not to be hindered, laid down, put down, to be made less than in any shape, way, or form, but for you to stand into your empowerment.

We see you in previous lifetimes, dear one, as a physical female embodying empowerment. We see you in what you would understand to be Goddess stature; we see you as a medicine woman who knew all herbal supplements and all herbal aspects of healing. You understood the stars and the moon in many lifetimes. You understood the ways in which the vibrations of the earth vibrated and when to and when not to do things. You listened to an inner compass, you were a scientist, you could say, in what you would understand to be Lemuria. You held office of your own in court, meaning you were truly a high priestess and a goddess, so aspects of you that have been are calling you forward in this lifetime because you did not do all of that to

*be here now, shrinking, and—though that is part
of the plan until you wake yourself up enough.*

The whole idea of entities coming in through a channel
to talk to me was quite fantastical, and I knew that many
would find these messages hard to believe, yet I did—and
still do—believe that there is much reality involved. My
strongest conviction lay in the observations that Grace
couldn't have been faking this session or making this stuff
up on the spur of the moment. To do this would involve the
height of cynicism or self-delusion. Grace's optimism filled
her, so much so that she infused others around her with it.
And she was certainly not some off-the-grid weirdo. Far
from being delusional, she was a lovely, well-spoken, professional woman. Grace and I had never met or talked before. She knew nothing of my life, yet Osairah's descriptions
resonated deeply with me.

The feeling of being a healer and an herbal medicine
woman ran strong through my entire being; it felt natural,
as if I'd come home. But the part about shrinking was like
being doused with cold water and pixie dust at the same
time—the shock of truth, yet also empowering.

Every romantic relationship that I have chosen has
been with men who attempted to squash my joy and divert
my passions. I did indeed shrink. That is exactly what I did,
and I faltered over the years, believing the harsh words, in-
sults, and put-downs from so many men. Their heartless attempts at subjugation now seem to me as if they believed
that chasing me off my path was essential to forging ahead
on what they saw as their own path. The memory of a particular scene often haunts me from the past. I was twenty-
eight years old and married to my ex-husband. I recalled
standing in the kitchen in our apartment as he bellowed at
me about my acting career. "WHEN ARE YOU GOING TO

GIVE UP? THIS IS RIDICULOUS YOU WILL NEVER MAKE IT!"

I also remembered the sting of hurt and anger when my live-in boyfriend—who ultimately kicked me in the shins—would refuse to turn on the answering machine (this was the 80's) so that I would miss calls from my agent for auditions. When I did have an audition, he would pick a fight right before I was to leave so that I would be in tears. He would do anything that he could to sabotage me.

Over the years I often wondered why people—men in particular—would become so angry when I attempted to pursue my interests. After having lived in Iran in 1978 with my family, I love the Persian language. I went to high school there. Over the years, I have studied it with professors and through books and CDs. Seeming to offer love, every man I have been with was absolutely furious about my interest in Persian. Perhaps past life issues were working themselves out, or perhaps it was the same dynamic as with the childhood bullies. My mates didn't have the same fire in their souls I had, and they wanted to snuff mine out, or replace it with themselves. And I allowed it.

Yes, I stumbled, tripped and even fell down the path, but I continued to follow the breadcrumbs and turn over every stone, as Rouben said. The fire in my soul has overpowered the negative agendas of others...with one possible exception.

"Osairah," I asked the entity visiting Grace, "can you take a look at my previous timelines with my husband Adolfo? We have an intense love and passion for each other, but equally intense power struggles. Always the caretaker, Adolfo often treats me more like his rebellious daughter than his wife. I am curious what past life karma we need to clear this time around?"

Hmmm, yes, we see many lifetimes with Adolfo. We see five previous lifetimes that are important to this lifetime. You have been brother and sister, mother-son, and lovers.

There are two themes very strong in connection to this lifetime, you have come together to save each other.

You were in what you would know as the country called Ireland. We are recognizing you as the physical female. You were but a very young girl; you had been sold from your family. This was a very difficult lifetime; there are many purposes for it, though. We recognize that lifetime as what you would say, a very painful time in history; there were many, many human beings that were sold into slavery, and we are recognizing this for you. You were actually bought by him. He was seventeen years older than you; you were bought at a very young age; you were twelve years old, and we see the painfulness of this lifetime.

And yet you grew into a certain kind of responsibility for him, because there was something in you about survival in that time. You knew you needed him as much as he was an owner of you. There are many conflicting energies of emotions, in that lifetime with him.

At the same time, dear one, one of the aspects of you in that lifetime, you definitely carried seventh dimensional energy light codes; you were in a sense very radiant, and even in the atrocity of it all, you were a beautiful being, and that was seen. He paid handsomely, you could say, for you. That radiance from you was a code of light within the seventh dimension that you brought forward, and you intersected, and you came together in that lifetime to heal many of the previous lifetimes that you had had.

There was huge regret that was healed through this dimensional connection with the two of you in the third dimension in that lifetime. We know that is difficult to understand given the circumstances. But there are far more complications as you realize in a lifetime of an energetic exchange, more emotion, and more previous timelines that are working themselves out.

Even though he knew on some level the way about the whole thing was wrong, he energetically put toward you a level of trust, meaning he granted you to have more of an equal partnership as you grew older, and it was because of this light that you carried that he put toward you this equal partnership. As we see you developing as a young woman and as one who in some senses was simply trying to survive a very bad situation, you became empowered in that situation as he gave you more trust.

And you began to energetically love him, which gave him more of a sense of—we will use the word safety with you—but this was quite the complicated life experience. We see to say, the reason we tell you that aspect of that lifetime, there is a thread—or we often refer to it as a channel-antenna—that connects to this lifetime and your relationship dynamic now. There are those factors that are being healed and literally dissipated by the actions you will take this day forward.

Most likely along with most of the world population, I knew that Adolfo would think this was complete hogwash. But honestly, I thought and still think this explanation is a huge possibility. That certainly made sense that in this life, Adolfo would be taking the role of running things, my advisor and my protector, a spillover from previous timelines. And since the past present and future are all existing simultaneously, it makes sense that our relationship would have shades of the Ireland timeline in it as well. All I had to do was take a different path from this day forward. What that entailed I was much less clear about.

I couldn't resist asking Osairah about my Macie, my furry best friend, and the brightest light in my life. "I found her on a street corner," I admitted to Osairah, "and we've been virtually inseparable ever since."

> *Macie, is very connected to you and loves you so strongly, she has been with you before in many lifetimes. Her devotion has been extraordinary, as both a physical human being as a female—not only a dog, because the consciousness of dog is love, compassion, devotion, and forgiveness. The loyalty and the devotion that she has had in many lifetimes with you, she is a soul home for you, a soul family member.*

The timer that Grace had set went off and the Osairah entities gave me their closing words.

> *We see to tell you that the lifetime that we spoke of in the ninth dimensional frequency of Pleiades and where you sit high council, dear one, you are in a frequency that is very strong to pull*

you forward, so there is that higher aspect of you. Wisdom keeper we see, who is helping to adjust, guide, intuit, push into your reality certain things. Pay attention to the signs. And we say to you that it is your highest aspects to call you into this lifetime you're your soul's development, not what you can gain or get. You will always be taken care of. The most important thing is the soul growth; it is vital to the transition team that you are on. So listen within. And know what we see is the reflection, what we see is the utmost beauty and grace, what we see is the honor that we must give you for the benevolent nature of your soul. We so enjoyed our conversation, and we so enjoyed the energetic exchange, dear one. You beam. Be the beamer that you are, beam brightly, navigate the waters for you are a great captain. We look forward to more. There is so much more waiting for you, and we look forward to being a part of that joy with you. We feel that we have been with you lifetime after lifetime, so it is so very good to see you on the third dimensional plane of this reality, and we wish you a magical adieu!

About five seconds later, Grace opened her eyes. She did not recall anything that was said, so we chatted a bit about the session. She told me that she would send me the recording on an MP3 within a few days. On the drive home, I let what had just transpired sink in. If this was real—and I believed that it was—how could I worry about, get upset, or doubt anything again? Knowing that I had lived thousands of lifetimes, and that there are more to come, on other dimensions, gave me a sense of calm. There is no rush to get everything done because apparently the saying, "you only live once" requires the phrase "in this dimensional frequency." We actually have all of eternity to play out each and every scenario. On the other hand, a lifetime is too precious to waste, and I would like to get my relationship with Adolfo right in this go round. I vowed to be more compassionate regarding his concerns and quirks, the deeper issues he carries. There is a deep love there, and we are all working out our karmic kinks.

This relieved so much stress that I had unknowingly allowed into each encounter with Adolfo and other conflicted relationships—the stress of thinking *I've only got a limited time to achieve my goals, and you're in my way*. I could back off from that, but I had to get this dynamic right with the person closest to me if I felt drawn to the energy of helping to heal others.

You Can Run But You Cannot Hide

*"Yet I am not more sure that my soul lives, than I am that perverse-
ness is one of the primitive impulses of the human heart — one of
the indivisible primary faculties, or sentiments, which give direction
to the character of Man."* ~ *Edgar Allan Poe*

Tauheedah had put together a healing team at the Imagine
Center and told me one night that she thought I was ready
to practice healing people, and would I like to participate in
the Tuesday night sessions? Each half-hour experience required two practitioners at a client cost of $50.00 and took
place in the back room of the center. Tauheedah provided
the table, candles, sage and incense, but practitioners
brought their own healing tools of choice. She said the healing room was a porthole for high vibrational entities from
all dimensions to enter and assist in the healing work, and
I believed her. The feeling of love and well-being was pal-
pable there, as if by magic. The most wonderful thing about
being a healer is that when the Universal energy comes
through you to the client, the healer also receives healing
energy coursing through the body. You give a healing, you

get a healing. I always feel amazing after facilitating a healing session. So, did I want to be on a healing team? I was thrilled.

I was in the flow, meditating on a regular basis, working my magic at my altar. I sensed blue ray energy swirling at my throat chakra into the vortex of creation. I regularly called in abundance the way Tauheedah taught us.

> *Manifest, manifest golden light,*
> *Bring to me my divine birthright!*

I'd followed the breadcrumbs toward enlightenment, riding the waves of creativity, and making matches in a steady stream that paid the bills. Technically, I experienced the fulfillment I envisioned and affirmed, yet my spiritual world often clashed with my marriage—as I've been fretting about—and my work. I wanted my worlds to merge.

Several new clients had signed on for matchmaking services in the past couple of months, which was great, but one was another Texan, an oilman named Randy. Randy owned over a hundred oil and natural gas wells and was living large. The only thing missing was his soul mate. I introduced him to a sweet little honey in Dallas who wore her bleached blonde hair in an updo and her double Ds in a push-up bra. It was *yee-haw!* at first sight. The couple soon headed to the Bahamas on his private jet for a week of, um, soul-mating. *You're welcome, and may you find nirvana. Blow out all your chakras with an eruption of kundalini* (a special form of energy that rises snake-like from the base of the spine and includes sexuality and personal power.)

I was happy for them, of course, but this wasn't the kind of meaningful spiritual endeavor I craved. Not only that, but one of my introductions—that of Jeremy to Miranda, the sugar-baby—still haunted me. I hadn't found a replacement for Miranda when I received a text from Jeremy.

> Hi Marla, I have been spending some time in Vancouver, working on a new book. I will be headed to Hong Kong soon to direct an Indie film based on my first book. This is exciting stuff, but I am basically running away from Miranda to the opposite end of the earth. We have had the craziest relationship. We kept trying to make things work, but it was destroying me. Faithfulness was my big issue. She feels that if she has sex with someone for money, it counts as work, and she is still being faithful. She told me she would only give up other men if I supported her financially. She then took a trip to Dubai with the sole purpose of meeting a billionaire. She did, but after a week they didn't get along. She then asked me to fly her home but would only fly first class. I wouldn't do it for a number of reasons. Unfortunately, I am still in love with her, wishing I wasn't. Trying to forget about her has been difficult, if not impossible. If Hong Kong isn't far enough away, I'll volunteer for a Mars expedition. ~ Jeremy.

Oh, the poor guy. I felt about as low as a wad of hot gum stuck to the bottom of a shoe. I'd single-handedly destroyed this wonderful man's life, at least for the past few months. I contemplated refunding his money, although he hadn't asked for it, and matters of the heart *were* risky business, even for seasoned professionals such as *moi*. And he did meet several nice gals before I matched him with the covert sexual self-merchandiser.

I was trying not to judge Miranda, in case any of my friends from the angelic dimension were looking over my shoulder.

Luckily, Jeremy's membership was a short program on the lower price point and not the year-long $15,000 membership that I usually offered. I prayed that he resisted having any contact with her from Hong Kong, because nowadays with email, text, Skype, Facetime, and other social media, you can run but you cannot hide.

I responded to his text.

> ~ Jeremy, I feel just awful. If it wasn't for me, you never would have met Miranda. I am so sorry.

His response came immediately.

> ~ Marla, don't feel bad about Miranda. I learned quite a bit from the experience.

Well, that was an interesting way to look at it. It would be nice, though, if adults, especially over the age of forty, no longer required a two-by-four smack in the head to drive a lesson home. We are all learning and evolving—often times all the way to the grave and back around for another go of it. As I learned in my session with Osairah, after many lifetimes together, Adolfo and I are still stepping on each other's rakes and getting smacked in the face with the handle.

Even though I wish I could make perfect matches every time, or at least matches that won't rip someone's heart out, I do know that is not possible. When dealing with the public, with hearts, souls, feeling, and egos, the dance is often delicate. Both Jeremy and Miranda have their soul contracts to complete in this third dimension, and I'd like to believe that I rotated into their energy field to bring them together for an advanced lesson. Jeremy is learning boundaries the hard-but-sure way, and Miranda was given the chance to learn that love does not have a price tag, that a precious human heart and a man's dignity is worth far more than a new refrigerator, a first class plane ticket, and a bedroom in the high-rent district.

Yet such experiences made me constantly worry that in providing guys like Randy with an instant "soul mate" or that inadvertently setting up a true heart like Jeremy for failure while receiving a good paycheck tended to link me to the Miranda energy. Edgar Allan Poe might say that Miranda's perversity typifies and defines the human character, but she also defined Jeremy's character in a positive way. He has indeed learned how vital and therefore precious faithfulness is.

I dropped another breadcrumb in my basket and tried to convince myself that I was a spiritual catalyst for powerful heart lessons.

I'd recently watched videos of a young woman named Teal Swan who actually describes herself professionally as a spiritual catalyst. I always got a boost in confidence while watching interviews of her on YouTube and felt that if Teal could overcome all the experiences she has gone through—like something out of a horror film—I could definitely transcend my lesser problems.

When she was a small child, Teal's parents, who were both Wilderness Rangers, accepted a job in the Wasatch-Cache National Forest of Utah, not knowing at the time about the cults and intensely religious climate of the location. The local community felt either threatened or diabolically attracted to Teal's psychic and extrasensory abilities. It was because of these talents that a family acquaintance, under the guise of mentorship, inducted her into a bizarre satanic cult. The man also held prominence in a Christian sect but was actually a psychopath with multiple personalities who ritualistically raped and tortured her as well as conditioning her with shock treatments—among many other atrocities—for thirteen years. She managed to escape from the cult when she was nineteen years old. Since then, Teal has become a "spiritual catalyst," both accepting and utilizing her abilities in order to teach people how to find hope in the midst of even the most extreme circumstances.

There are hundreds of videos of Teal, many of which are conducted through a YouTube channel by non-professionals who act as a host of their own show. Many did fantastic jobs, but the one I chose that day—one I hadn't already seen—featured a guy who apologized at the beginning for his "newbie status." Others had also faltered or allowed long awkward pauses, didn't know what question to ask next, or were just plain boring. I heard my small inner voice say, *You can do just as well, Marla, if not better than this! What are you waiting for?*

I had been sending in tapes of my TV interviews for several years, hoping for a spot as a reality show hostess for dating, but these spiritual interviews were free and truly helped people. This new direction might be my true calling or at least lead to it. I selected another video of Teal by a terrific interviewer, Joanna DeVoe, a perky, quirky, delightful blonde with a luminous complexion and sparkly blue eyes. Joanna was known as The Kick Ass Witch. (She puts the "K" in Magick!) And she looked like she was having so much fun. After watching Joanna's interview, I decided then and there that I would start my own YouTube interview show, chatting with experts in all subjects from matchmakers, psychics, sex therapists, mediums, authors, and more. Hey, Larry King moved from Prime Time to YouTube...

Amazingly, Adolfo jumped right in and helped me to order and download *call recorder* software for recording Skype interviews. He even composed a piece of music to use as my intro song. I picked out a logo and a name for the show—*Conversations With Cupid*. I emailed Joanna to praise her interview skills and found out that she also lived in Los Angeles. We met for lunch, and she agreed to be my first guest. Bingo Boingo...I became a talk show host!

Caution: May Be Habit-Forming

*"Everyone should carefully observe which way his heart draws him,
and then choose that way with all of his strength."*
~ Hasidic Proverb

I'm Marla, and I'm an addict. Well, not to anything like alcohol or drugs, not to Big Macs, diet coke, sex, or working out. Not even to chocolate. Earning New Age certifications provides my fix. I got such an empowerment rush from qualifying for my crystal healing and Reiki certifications that I felt a little empty without them as a focus in my life. They provided a badly needed distraction from frustrating and disempowering matchmaking hassles and spousal tiffs. So, if all addictions are attempts at self-medication, I was creating emotional and spiritual highs—with, presumably, corresponding endorphins in the brain—through these wonderful classes. But then what?

Fortunately, through the Internet, far more modality options are available than ever before. I carefully reviewed websites and reading material, an essential step because there are many out there who seem to be on ego-trips or greed trips or both. I found a contact that seemed right for me and started taking online courses in Life Force Energy Healing.

The person offering these classes was Master healer/shaman, Deborah King. Deborah is a Hay House author with a radio show, and, like Teal Swan, had endured a traumatic childhood of sexual abuse. Her mother despised and resented her, and her father molested her from the time she was a toddler until the age of twelve, including raping her at age nine. The local parish priest, to whom her father confessed, also sexually abused Deborah. Later, as a successful attorney in her twenties, Deborah masked her childhood traumas with drug and alcohol addictions as well as risky sexual behavior until a medical diagnosis changed her life.

Cervical cancer forced her to evaluate her lifestyle and issues from her past. Hoping to avoid surgery or chemo treatments, Deborah decided to try alternative medicine first and met with an energy healer. She experienced a miraculous remission on the table of the healer. Excited about the seeming miracle, she asked, *what is this power, and how can I share it with others?* Part of her answer lay in traveling the globe to meet other shamans and healers, spending hour after hour in meditation, and living among animals and nature. I was so taken with her knowledge and approach that I pushed Adolfo's voice to the recesses of my mind, the one lecturing me with, *Marlita, this is exactly why you don't have more money saved for retirement.* I breezed through four levels of her teachings with a certification for each level. I couldn't absorb the material fast enough. I also became certified in her Angels of Energy Healing Course and her Chakra Wisdom Course.

One day on Deborah's radio show, she announced that she would be holding a two- hour afternoon seminar at *The Center for Spiritual Living* in Westlake Village, which was just thirty minutes from my house. It was warm in late June, but the green summer leaves on the tall trees offered shady walkways in a crowded professional center. I arrived early and got a good seat inside a small auditorium. Deborah's seminars begin with a talk, and then she selects people to come up on stage where she actually performs healing work right there in front of everyone. The person remains standing, and Deborah assesses their chakras and energy field with her hands, and then continues the energy work, removing blockages and shifting the energy.

One of the most exciting things that she does at her events is to initiate people, a process of connecting back to Source, level by level. I knew from listening to her radio show that those deemed ready for initiation are usually active in their spiritual practice, meditating regularly, or doing energy work, thereby providing an energetic base in order to advance the person to a higher level. First and second level initiations are very subtle, and most people are not even aware of having them. Beyond the second level, a facilitator is almost always required.

There were about a hundred people at the event, and I grabbed a seat in the center about four rows back. Deborah gave a short talk before calling people up on stage. Her explanation went something like this:

Energy flows through us and around us at all times. In fact, every single thing you see, hear, and touch is comprised of this invisible current, including your own body. Mystics call it life force, while scientists study its movements through heat and light variations, but no matter how you quantify it, this energy is the source and building block of all life on Earth.

I desperately wanted to be selected to come up on stage just to be near Deborah and experience her energy, but I wasn't sick, worried, or depressed, so what reason could I use to go up and get a healing? Being addicted and obsessed with certificates probably wasn't a condition she'd want to heal.

The only thing that had been bothering me was the pain in my ankles. They'd been hurting for months, especially at night, and I couldn't figure out what the problem was. When getting up to go the bathroom at night, I had to hobble like an old woman. Over the months I had thought about what could be causing the pain. I'd decided that from a spiritual/energetic standpoint, I wasn't feeling supported by Adolfo in my interests, and that could be weighing me down, causing my ankles to bear too much of the burden of support. This self-diagnosis made me feel quite the spiritual adept, but actually, it was probably just early arthritis.

Throughout the two hours, I enthusiastically raised my hand every time she was ready for another person to come up, but no luck. What? Was I invisible? At least I would have a chance to briefly meet her after the event downstairs in the gift shop where she would be signing books, but I was quite disappointed not to be selected. Then right before the event was coming to a close, she looked out into the audience and pointed at me.

"You are ready to initiate! Come on up."

I was stunned. I looked at the women sitting on both sides of me to make sure it was really me that she was pointing to.

"Yes, you. Come on up."

I hustled as fast as I could up to the stage in a bit of a daze because I hadn't allowed myself to imagine I was ready to be initiated by Deborah King! I was ecstatic. All of my spiritual work must have paid off.

I stood next to her facing the audience, and she placed her left hand behind my back and commenced to scan my energy field with her right hand. She moved her hand up and down in front of my body and then outwards as if she was playing with my energy and releasing it to the heavens.

As she moved her hand outwards she exclaimed, "Oh my! Look at that, it's sparkly and angelic! It's beautiful!"

Her facial expression made her seem like she was seeing my brand of energy for the first time. Suddenly, in a high clear voice, she broke out in operatic song.

"Aaaauhhhhhhhhhhhhhhhhhhhhh...."

Her sustained note raised goose bumps from my neck to my toes. I shed tears of joy. I could feel the angelic presence as energy shifted. Deborah and I hugged each other, and I returned to my seat. On the way to the gift shop, people were calling out to me, "hey, angel, congratulations!"

I wafted along on an angelic cloud. Twenty minutes later, in the gift shop I handed Deborah her book, *Entangled In Darkness* to sign, and she hugged me and congratulated me. I asked her if the initiation was permanent.

"Yes, it will stay with you," she said.

I told her that I was in her online Life Force Energy Healing Course. "That is wonderful," she said. "I would love to work with you, keep it up."

"Oh, I will. And thank you again," I gushed.

On my way home, I could barely concentrate on traffic, so I stopped by The Healing Tree for a hot herbal tea and some dried mushrooms. You eat them like delicious little vegetable chips. At twelve dollars for a tiny bag, they were definitely a luxury item. I ignored Adolfo's imagined reaction—*twelve dollars for a few mushrooms? Come on!*

It was nice to see Dr. Moe again. I explained why I hadn't continued with the percussion therapy. "I really thought it was beneficial, but my husband was just too upset about it. Seeing the bruises really freaked him out. My mother as well as my BFF, Julie, also thought I had lost my mind. I guess not everyone is as open minded as I am," I said.

"I understand, Marla. It is definitely a specialized therapy, and is not for everyone."

"But I must tell you, I am still surprised that the reaction from my friends and family were so negative. I mean, it's my body. After all, people do *rolfing* to forcefully release knots of bad energy. I've heard it can be quite painful, and look at the pain and agony many people go through to have plastic surgery such as breast implants and face-lifts. Hey, that's no picnic. That seems like it would be absolute torture to me!"

Dr. Moe nods in commiseration. "They're willing to go through the pain because they think the end result is worth it."

"Dr. Moe, I have a great idea. I'm doing a YouTube show called, *Conversations With Cupid.* I would love to interview you about this modality. You can explain exactly what it is and the benefits. Maybe we can change some minds, who knows?"

Dr. Moe agreed and asked me to email him to set a date to record the interview.

This was turning out to be an amazing day. I deserved and bought an extra bag of freeze-dried mushrooms.

When I got home, I went into my sanctuary and lit a candle. I pulled one of my talking boards out of the closet and set the stage in my usual spot on the floor with my crystals and saints placed around it. I had been diligent in trying to get the board to work on my own for the past few months. Every evening I had given it about ten minutes before giving up.

I watched a video on YouTube made by a guy with a cool Scottish accent, explaining how to use the board solo. He said, "it can take up to twenty or thirty minutes for it to start moving, so please be patient, and don't just rule it off. Your arms *will* get sore; nobody said communicating with the dead was going to be easy. No pain no gain."

That was for sure. Not only did my arms get fatigued but my back was aching.

Julie had been a great sport, coming over every week or two so that I could chat with Murth. Accompanied by Julie, I summoned Murth, who continued to spell out the reason I couldn't get it to move by myself. My energy hadn't been right yet. I really wanted to speak to Murth without having to bother Julie, but I needed another person's positive energy. I'd even tried to get creative, enticing Macie to set her paw on the planchette to give it her sweet little doggie energy, but she looked puzzled as she cocked her head, willing only to sit next to me and watch.

I did feel lighter after my initiation, different, I guess, kind of spacey, yet filled with appreciation for my surroundings, my life, my adorable Macie beside me. I recited my protection prayers and invocation and placed my fingers on the planchette.

"Hello, is anyone here that would like to communicate with me?" I began as usual.

Ten seconds in, the planchette began to move. HOLY CANNOLI!

H-E-L-L-O M-A-R-L-A

"Hello, who is this please?

M-U-R-T-H

"Murth, I can finally talk to you by myself! I am so happy."

M-E T-O-O. I L-O-V-E Y-O-U M-A-R-L-A

"I love you too, Murth. Hey, Murth, am I on the right track with all of the healing work I am doing? What do you see for me?"

Y-O-U A-R-E O-N T-H-E R-I-G-H-T T-R-A-C-K. S-T-A-Y F-O-C-U-S-E-D.

G-O-D L-O-V-E-S Y-O-U.

"Murth, what do you look like?

I A-M T-A-L-L

"Is there any way I can see you?"

Y-O-U W-I-L-L S-E-E M-E S-O-O-N.

"How can I see you? What should I do?"

M-E-D-I-T-A-T-E

Murth and I chatted for an hour until my back hurt too much and I had to stop.

Luckily stubbornness is one of my qualities. Over the next few weeks, I spoke with Murth everyday even if it was only for five minutes, enough to enjoy getting to know each other. She also introduced me to my second angel in command, Thomas. Thomas often came in on the board before Murth and his energy was different than hers. Thomas was a bit more formal, *Yes, hello Marla, Angel Thomas here, how are you?* as opposed to Murth who would say things like, *hello Marla, this is your badass angel, Murth.* She had a great sense of humor.

Thomas would sign off with, goodbye, have a nice evening, and Murth would usually say, *go to bed and get some rest. Angel kisses xoxo.*

Once I started feeling confident in my solo talking board skills, I decided to try my hand at contacting someone that I didn't know. Someone famous. I am a fan of Edgar Allan Poe. I was curious to see if I could bring him in on the board. I meditated, and asked if he would come in, and...

Yes Marla, Edgar Allan Poe here.

Me: Is this really Edgar?

Poe: Yes, this is Poe.

Me: You know that I am fascinated by you, right?

Poe: Yes, I love that about you.

Me: Did you ever have an affair with Frances Osgood?

Poe: Yes, I did have an affair with Frances. Loved her deeply. I had a hard time in life on earth. Very poor, a mad, lonely existence.

Me: Where were you born?

Poe: Boston.

Me: What city did you die in?

Poe: Baltimore.

Me: How did you end up walking the streets of Baltimore?

Poe: Wet. It was raining. I was not drunk or crazy like they said.

Me: Can we write a poem together?

Poe: Yes.

Me: Okay, go ahead, I will write it down.

A Mad, Lonely, Life
By "Edgar Allan Poe"

A mad lonely life, made a life by a man
Who loved with a love but could not make love
To the woman he adored.
Big mistake to ever make.
Man is only flesh and bone.

Man loves. Man bites off a bit more than he can chew.
A man is a lover of many things, interesting things.
Big mistake in store for man;
Lovers are many but angels are few.
Yancy is a man lost in his dreams
But he will be knowingly called to fight.
Big anguish awaits him but he will endure.
A lost soul better make peace with himself before a cold death.
A man is not but a soul, a man is God made many times over.
Man is made in the image of love and light,
But bones are made of terror.
Love is eternal, don't worry my dear.

I was quite impressed with the poem despite the glaring cliché of *biting off more than he could chew*, the contemporary use of "big mistake" and the unknown *Yancy*. It certainly lacked Poe's precision with language and his perfectly metered rhyme. It wasn't fantastic, yet I thought that it evoked Poe, and I loved the whole section that ended with "a man is God made many times over."

I naturally had doubts that the entity really was Poe. If souls reincarnate, Poe would probably have lived several other lifetimes by now. Or did a remnant of Poe energy still exist and package itself in a more current form? The overall beauty of the poem made it worthy, so "trickster" energy didn't seem to be involved. Whoever this spirit poet was, he did make the effort to collaborate with me so I could get a poem down on paper. I found that amazing in itself.

I felt different as I lay in bed that night, as if my spirit were dancing with angels. I felt expanded and caught myself smiling alone in the darkness. I couldn't say exactly what had changed, but I knew I never wanted to reclaim the flat, trudging, fearful weight I carried before I started this enlightenment process. Yes, I felt light. I was Marla—lite.

I would try not to be too obsessed, but I wanted still more.

Caution: Spiritual Power May Become Invasive

"Animal lovin' ain't shovin' 'em in the oven."
~ Harley Johnstone, aka Durianrider

I'd found a trove of inner strength—available to us all—from the knowledge that I possess the power of connection to the eternal world of Source, avatars, angels, ancestors, past lives, life force energies, and more. I felt spiritually and psychologically uplifted. I felt light-hearted, yet I also felt protected. And all this was playing out in ways that surprised me.

That protected feeling is wonderful, but it isn't something to be taken for granted. It is a constant process, as I would be learning the hard way. When Julie forwarded me an email from Meetup.com that a young woman named Kerri was giving fifteen-minute angel readings for twenty bucks at a place in Canoga Park called Freak's Antiques, I couldn't resist. What better way to spend a couple of hours on a Saturday?

I felt like I was in Elvira's parlor or something. The cozy little nook where Kerri gave the readings was witchy and magical. There were inspirational writings on the walls, a human skeleton, a child's coffin, religious artifacts, a candelabra, and various paintings and statuettes of saints. In the back of the curiosity shop, I stepped through the purple crushed velvet curtains, leaving Julie to shop while I sat across from Kerri, a cute redhead. She'd adorned a small round table with a candle, a few crystals, and a couple of angel statuettes for a nicely protected reading. Focusing on my career, Kerri said that I was in the flow, and that I would continue to attract new clients. *May it be so.*

Julie then disappeared behind the curtains while I browsed around the shop. It was chock full of fascinating antique oddities. A basket of doll heads from the 1800's, mannequin hands and fingers, a mummified spider monkey, a taxidermied pintail duck with a puppet head screwed on, a post mortem fingerprint kit, a vintage physician's bag, a vintage ventriloquist doll, homemade beeswax candles, framed photos of Edgar Allan Poe, and variety of books on Poe. I spotted an Edgar Allan Poe coffee mug. Score! He'd be coming home with me.

Up near the cash register was the piece de resistance! A table with a Ouija board painted on the top. An impulse, without reciting a prayer of protection, I placed my fingers on the planchette, and asked if anyone would like to communicate. It started to move.

Poe here. Hello.

Hey, my old friend! Is this really Poe?

Yes. I am Poe.

I wanted to chat with him more, but Julie emerged from behind the curtain. Darn. I mentally bid farewell to Edgar and paid for my mug. If the spirit really was Poe—or some essence of Poe—it may not have been strong enough to resist other low level trickster entities that hung around, looking for openings. But I didn't really understand that then because I was so amazed at the positive aspects of spirituality—the side that enables authentic power.

I tend to be a peaceful person, generally doing whatever it takes to avoid a confrontation, so I had no idea that my new spirituality had built up new boundaries that demanded dignity and respect. A client named Brad, an introverted accountant, had been sending me snarky, passive-aggressive emails and texts for over a month, and, although hurt and upset, I had calmly tried to reason with him. This apparently gave him the notion that he could rudely boss me around, and I would just have to take it.

So when I got sick, which was very rare, I'd caught a cold that kicked my ass so hard, I couldn't get out of bed for five days. I work from home and am not exposed to viruses in the workplace, but at the restaurant where Adolfo works, someone is always sick whether staff or customer. I think he brought home a potent bug. I emailed each of my clients to let them know what was going on and apologized for any inconvenience. I still managed to take my laptop to bed with me, however, and sent out some profiles for a few of my male clients, including Brad. Most clients only signed up for one to two introductions per month, so a week was not the end of the world for any of them.

When I was well enough to be back at my desk on a Monday morning, there was an email I hadn't opened from Brad.

OH PLEASE, NO EXCUSE. ONCE I WAS AS SICK AS YOU WERE, AND I STILL WORKED. MY CLIENTS HAD NO IDEA I WAS SICK. SO I DON'T WANT TO HEAR IT!

I took a deep breath, decided I'd had enough of this abuse and didn't have to tolerate it. I sent him an email.

Maybe you think that I should end up in the hospital with pneumonia because you want a date? Brad, when you send me snarky, rude texts, and speak to me in a rude manner, do you realize that I am a person at the other end of the email or phone? I have feelings. I take great pride in my work, and have for over a decade!

The phone rang almost immediately. Brad calling, of course, yelling.

"ALL I KNOW IS THAT I DON'T HAVE A DATE THIS WEEK! AND LAST MONTH YOU WERE ON VACATION!"

"What? I don't deserve to have a life? Yes, I took a week off last month, which had ZERO effect on your matches, since you were still dating Elsa at the time; and after you two broke up, I had another match ready for you right away. I don't need to have my ass sitting over in the San Fernando Valley every minute for you to enjoy great service."

The man had definitely flipped my switch, and I barreled through before he could cut in. "You have NO IDEA

HOW TO TALK TO PEOPLE, and that is one of the reasons that you are still single at fifty-four years of age. You can't get it done on your own."

Whoa. Had I really just said that? I softened a tad in the icy silence.

"I am trying to help you, Brad, but your behavior is outrageous. Tell me how I'm supposed to get excited about matching you? How can I call up an attractive sought-after woman and say, *'Hey, I have this amazing guy named Brad. You just have to meet him!'* How can I do that when all I feel is a desire to dropkick you when you speak to me in such a mean-spirited way?"

He sputtered and coughed, but I think the nerve I struck had apparently sent shockwaves past his ego and straight to his heart chakra or higher self or something. Quietly, he said, "I... guess I didn't realize I was being rude... uh... sorry."

I assured him that I was indeed on the job and would be in touch very soon with more options.

I hung up as mega-hits of adrenaline and cortisol had set my heart hammering along with a flash of steamy heat on this late summer morning.

Had I actually yelled at a client? It was the first time I'd ever done that, and *wow*. It felt so *goooooood*! But I also had a case of jitters. After summoning such powerful chemistry, my whole system had zinged out of whack hormonally.

This was a case for Super Juice, aka *green gunk*! Except I was out of the good stuff that goes into it.

There is no doubt that my spiritual journey and raising my vibration through healing modalities and meditation has expanded to influence my whole life. One surprising way is that I have become extremely sensitive to environments. For example, walking into a mainstream super market, I find that the whole place feels and smells toxic. Only a small percentage of items are actually whole foods. The rest is processed "food stuff" filled with colorings, chemicals, GMOs, hormones, antibiotics, and other nasties. The non-food items, like cleaning and laundry products, are full of chemicals. I feel overwhelmed after a few minutes. However, walking into Whole Foods Market is a vastly different experience. The smell of the place is that of farm fresh produce, exotic teas, heavenly coffee, spices, and organic cleansers. Its energy calms me.

As I filled my basket that day with organic kale, green apples, cucumbers, lemons, celery, and parsley for my "green gunk," I felt incredibly blessed. Even though many of my clients are high maintenance, I am grateful to them for providing me with the means to buy organic food and an especially exciting recent purchase, my Vitamix blender, used by chefs in restaurants. It's so high-powered, that the dates and nuts in my smoothies are actually all blended in, instead of little bits and chunks that have to be chewed.

Of course, we all need fiber, especially in carbs and proteins, but when it comes to juiced raw veggies, your digestive system doesn't have to work as hard to break it all down. So rather than relying on your molars to grind out the vitamins, minerals, and enzymes, juicing makes the nutrients more readily available to the body in much larger quantities.

I had put off purchasing my Vitamix for a couple of years because of the hefty price tag of seven hundred bucks, but then I found a $100 coupon. At first Adolfo freaked out. *Six hundred dollars for a blender? Have you lost your mind? We already have a blender! And a juicer!*

I proceeded to sit his butt down and showed him demos on YouTube that included black cherry chocolate vegan ice cream, made with a Vitamix. A dozen Facebook friends offered testimonials like, *It changed my life!* And, *If my house were on fire, the one thing I would grab is my Vitamix.* Many shared their favorite recipes. So Adolfo gave me the green light, and now I make incredible restaurant quality vegan delicacies in minutes: amazing smoothies, carrot ginger soup, hummus, vegan ice cream, almond milk, bread, and muffins. There is almost nothing that cannot be made with a Vitamix.

Actually, I've been juicing since the late 1990's when I was living in Chicago. A Peruvian woman named Carmen helped me with my chronic constipation. I persevered through a series of about twenty colonics, which sounds horrible, but was actually an amazing experience. I literally and emotionally let go of so much! Carmen taught me how to eat to heal myself and get things moving regularly, and she also told me to buy a juicer and drink beautiful fresh vegetables juices every day. I also cut out white flour and sugar. Things got better, and I continued juicing, but now, it's a total commitment, and I feel amazing. Nothing tastes better to me than a fresh green juice. And walking into a juice bar? A religious experience.

Though not all psychics and mediums are vegan or even vegetarian, for me, it is a package deal. It's about consciousness. Part of this consciousness simply reflects my love of animals. Like many middle-class kids, I grew up on t-bone steaks—I liked mine rare—pork chops, ground beef casseroles, chicken cacciatore, and boxes of Kentucky Fried Chicken with mashed potatoes, gravy, and biscuits, especially enjoyable from TV trays on Sunday afternoons while watching Tarzan on channel eleven with the family and acquiring a mustache of 2% milk drunk from the large glass that accompanied each meal.

However, at the age of about nine, I slowly realized that something was going on which no one was in any hurry for me to know about. Directly behind our back yard was a pasture of several acres that belonged to the Salmon family— nothing to do with any kind of fish. A barbed wire fence separated our property from the Salmon's who acquired four young steers every spring and raised them to adulthood. I loved petting the steers on the head, looking into their soulful big brown eyes softened with long eyelashes. I picked long, tender ferns from our yard, and offered them through the fence. Their heads pressed up to the barbed wire, and their long rough tongues lapped in the delicious foliage right from my hands, and they munched away.

I always became attached to the beautiful animals, sometimes naming them, only to find one day in the late fall that they had disappeared. That year I was nine, I was horrified to discover that the Salmons sold the steers for slaughter.

Over dinner one night, I said, "I don't think that was right to murder the steers, especially Maxwell and Freddie."

"Yeah," Dad said, "but you sure like eating that big juicy steak on your plate, don't you?"

Yes, I sure do, I thought, but still, something about it just wasn't right.

Then, in my senior year of high school, I took a class called "Single Survival" that taught us how to cook, grocery shop, and other skills that we would need to know as adults living on our own. The teacher showed us a poster with a picture of a steer on it only it had no skin, so we just saw the muscles. Each section bore the name of the cut, chuck, rib, round, flank, sirloin, brisket, and more. The teacher explained that we were actually eating the muscles of the animal. I had no idea that I was eating muscles. Seeing that animal reduced to cuts of muscle was so disturbing that I went off beef then and there.

In my late twenties, I married a French chef named Bruno. We went to France and stayed at his parents' home in the countryside. His father was also a chef, but to bring in extra money, his father also raised a few pigs, chickens, and sheep to sell for slaughter. Each evening I would carry out the scraps from our dinner to feed to the pigs. A neighbor also raised pigs yet on a larger scale. Enormous female pigs lay in cubicles in the barn with their babies. The farmer, Maurice, picked up one of the piglets and handed it to me. It was the sweetest little thing, all soft and pink with splotches of black. I kissed the piglet on its head, my heart breaking, knowing this beautiful, sentient creature would soon be killed and carved up. Similar experiences brought me to the understanding that I could not claim to love and care about animals and also eat them.

Most of us grew up eating meat, wearing leather, enjoying the circus and the zoo. We never considered the impact of these actions on the animals involved. Supporters of animal rights believe that animals have an inherent worth— a value completely separate from their usefulness to humans. So this brings me to my other level of consciousness that is in harmony with a vegan lifestyle, that of oneness with other beings—which definitely heightens my spiritual experiences.

Dogs and pigs have the same capacity to feel pain and similar intelligence, but it is prejudice that allows us to think of one animal as a companion and the other as dinner. I believe that every creature is given a will to live and has rights that exclude systematic cruelty. All animals have the ability to suffer in the same way and to the same degree that humans do. They feel pain, pleasure, fear, frustration, loneliness, friendship, and motherly love.

Ovo-lacto vegetarians (those who consume a diet containing milk, milk products, and eggs) may seem like an in-between option, but for me, this isn't acceptable because the competitive factory farming system causes such cruelty and suffering of the animals, I can't bear to even read about it. Yet, I can't ignore it and pretend that my spirituality is separate from the agony the animals must endure to produce what goes into my mouth. More and more, we learn that each emotion that humans and animals experience have corresponding biochemistry in the body, including eggs and milk products. Even if I were ignorant of the animals' suffering, do I need the additional chemistry of their stress in my food?

Mother earth is stressed as well. Animal activist Erin Janus who has assembled extensive research on this subject says:

> Animal agriculture is the leading cause of environmental damage. There is nothing destroying the earth (and rainforests) more than raising animals for consumption. A pig farm of 5,000 pigs for example, produces as much fecal waste as a city of 50,000 people. It's a total disgrace to the earth to eat animals at this time in history. The demand for meat and dairy (animal agriculture) is also the leading cause of water pollution, ocean dead-zones, habitat destruction, and greenhouse gas emissions. We are out of line with nature. There is more harm being done to the planet than good.

And then there are the vibes. Today's energy grids generate electromagnetic fields that are constantly around us though unknown to our ancestors. With the influx of fast food, sodas, microwave dinners, preservatives, and other low vibratory meals and snacks, we are contracting more cancer, diabetes, and heart diseases. Societies remain stuck in rigid religious dogmas, using what should be the highest form of connection to the eternal universal spirit to instead generate hate, conflict, and war. Many individuals turn atheist, losing all connection to the sacred Source entirely instead of opening to the beauty of quantum connections that may explain *chi*, the eternal *om*, the ancient *ankh*, the life force. The cleaner and less toxic your body is, the higher your vibrational frequency, and the more you are a clear channel for the higher energies. Your body truly is a temple.

I found it fascinating to read that psychic/medical intuitive Teal Swan, must watch her diet closely so as to not spontaneously astral project or channel at inopportune times. She needs to stay extremely grounded and therefore doesn't drink alcohol or take drugs. However, to keep her spiritual abilities in working order, she is a lifelong vegan, which doesn't stop her from also being an avid food lover and organic cook.

She senses energy fields and auras that change with the ingestion of foods. Energetically, she says the worst things you can put in your body are substitute sugars, such as saccharine, aspartame, and sorbitol, which can sometimes cause an energetic reaction worse than a response to heroin. The second worst tier includes anything with preservatives and pesticides. Third on the list of vibrational screwer-uppers is refined sugars/carbs which includes alcohol, white flour, sugar, corn syrups, and so forth. Margarines with trans fat is next, followed by dairy. She says she's never met a person that can handle dairy, even when they think they can.

I love this part, which is from one of Teal's YouTube videos:

When you go on a spiritual path, you will find that your physiology will resonate at a different level. That instantly means the more and more spiritual you get, certain foods will resonate or not resonate with you. This is the real reason why in a lot of spiritual circles, you will see the same kind of diets among what people would call spiritual masters. It is because they have ascended to a certain level where the only foods that are able to resonate with where they are—physically and mentally—are these certain kinds of foods. So..., if you are following the path to spirituality you will be naturally inspired to eat these types of foods.

I think of the quote from the great philosopher Pythagoras, "Men dig their graves with their own teeth, and die more by those instruments than by all weapons of their enemies."

Teal, Erin Janus, and others talk about an unsettling situation regarding the pineal gland. Through research into NDEs (near-death experiences) and dreaming, factual evidence is surfacing that seems to connect higher spiritual frequencies to the pineal gland. Philosophers and mystics have long pondered the pineal gland, beginning with the time of Galen, a Greek doctor practicing a hundred years before Christ. Later mystics came to see the pineal gland as the source of a higher inner vision, the third eye, which is associated with the brow chakra. The great philosopher Descartes called it the "seat of the soul." When activated, the pineal gland is said to become a direct line into higher states of consciousness. About the size of a pea, the pineal gland is located in the exact geometric center of the brain, directly behind the eyes and sits in a tiny cave behind and above the pituitary gland, "our gateway to other worlds."

Unfortunately, as we age, the pineal gland can become calcified, causing calcium phosphate to develop over the gland, sometimes called "brain sand." (Yikes.) For those of us that seek to fully activate our spiritual potential and tap into the power of the pineal gland, we must begin by strengthening its function through detoxification and proper nutrition. Diets loaded with the elements Teal identified, including fluoridated water in particular, leave the light-sensitive pineal gland (and the rest of the body) exposed to many more toxins than ever before. Many of us have a pineal gland that is already completely calcified.

Even though I could contact my angel guide Murth and other entities on my talking board, I still was not able to hear them clearly, or get psychic messages or visions. So, in case I had brain sand, I immediately cut fluoride out by replacing my toothpaste with a fluoride-free formula and, of course, drinking only filtered water. My pineal gland cleansing spree also equaled a spending spree because the supplements I researched on the Internet to loosen the grit in my third eye added up to a tidy sum. But they now sit in my kitchen cabinet:

Oregano oil

Neem extract

Chaga mushroom

Raw cacao

Iodine

Raw apple cider vinegar

Melatonin

Spirulina powder

I'll let you know when my channel opens wider.

So, juicing and experimenting with my Vitamix to make smoothies and soups, I progressed along on my journey. My YouTube show, "Conversations with Cupid," was gathering hits and becoming a major passion. I was interviewing so many fascinating experts and posting two to three videos per week. One particularly sparkly guest was Steffany Barton, a nurse, turned medium and angel communicator. With her luminous eyes and a smile that revealed her perfect white teeth, she exuded peace and angelic energy. Several days after her interview, Steffany was generous enough to offer me a reading via Skype. The first thing she told me was that my dad was there with me. I was astonished.

She could see him and she told me that he was so proud of me and was always with me. I was on the verge of tears when she started to giggle.

"Your dad is saying, 'Enough with the blending! Food is meant to be eaten, not drunk.'"

This was totally my dad's personality, the way he teased me.

"So you make a lot of the healthy stuff?" Steffany asked.

"Right. Green gunk." I described my concoctions.

My dad was teasing me from the other side of existence, but the moment held a tinge of sadness. I always worked out and ate healthy back when Dad was eating donuts for breakfast and going to the Country Buffet, loading his plate with calorie-laden foods, and then going back for the desserts. He also smoked and drank, the total opposite from me in that way. I had often tried to get him into juicing and eating healthy, but it just wasn't going to happen.

The thing that broke my heart was when my dad was in the hospital and had just gotten the news from the cold-hearted doctor, stiffly informing him that his cancer was terminal. I was sitting next to him on the edge of his bed, our feet dangling off the side. He looked down at the floor and said, "Can I have some of your juice?"

There comes a point when it's just too late for many people. However, I watched a fantastic documentary, "Fat, Sick, and Nearly Dead," which follows the sixty-day journey of an Australian man named Joe Cross as he follows a juice fast to regain his health under the care of a doctor in the US. Following his fast and the adoption of a plant-based diet, Joe lost a hundred pounds and was able to discontinue all medications. His story inspired me to give a juice fast a try, and I made it to five days. Fasting is an interesting experience, as not only toxins are released, but old patterns and ways of thinking can also come up and be released. It is a time for reflection and healing.

Here's a little wellness shot I do almost daily in my juicer. I just love it and feel amazing. Here's what I use for a three-ounce portion of juice:

Turmeric Root

ginger

Green apple

Lemon

10 drops of oregano oil

Sprinkle of cayenne pepper

Okay, so I am putting this authenticity out there, especially my dream to stay in a twenty-one day retreat and do a juice fast/cleanse. Who's with me?

Kindred Spirits or Loony Toons?

"My religion consists of a humble admiration of the illimitable superior spirit who reveals himself in the slight details we are able to perceive with our frail and feeble mind." ~ Albert Einstein

Hammer in hand, I took a step back to admire the four framed certificates on the wall above my desk, now proudly announcing my new skills.

Crystal Healing

Reiki, levels 1 & 2

Life Force Energy Healing Levels 1- 4

Levels 1, 2 & 3 of psychic development from the Eternal Light Foundation

That last one was taught by Grace Cavanaugh and Osairah. (Yes, Osairah taught part of the class.) Years ago if someone had told me that one day I would be taking a psychic development class from a collective of twelve entities from other dimensions, well, let's just say I would probably have written them off as having partaken a little too much acid back in the '60s. Yet I had opened up to so many new possibilities, new entities, and dimensions, I was becoming a walking cosmic house party. These little slips of paper not only represented physical proof to me of the portal through which I could now pass, but also of my slow but steady persistence. If I wanted something powerfully enough, I held it within my co-creative powers with the universe to achieve it. Of course, energy healing and spiritual development are a lifelong endeavor, and I still had much to learn.

Adolfo wandered in, sipping a cup of coffee. Uh-oh, I thought, here comes the lecture on what a colossal waste of time and money this represented.

"Nice job; the certificates look good." He kissed me on the cheek. "I'm proud of you, *mi amor.*"

Whoa, had I accidentally stepped through yet another portal to an entirely alternate world? Was I somehow speaking to an illusion, or was this actually my darling husband that not so long ago had accused me of almost killing him with my energy, calling me "dangerous"?

"I mean it," he said. "I'm proud of you for all you have accomplished."

"Thanks, honey." Yes, he was casting shadows like a real person as he bent closer to read the titles. "I feel so professional with the certificates on the wall," I admitted to this solid entity who was so like my husband. "Like a doctor or something."

"I know I can be a jerk sometimes, and I don't mean to be."

At that point, I suspected I could walk through the illusion of walls around me.

He turned to look directly at me. "I just don't want you blowing money. I'm trying to protect our future. Be careful, we aren't that young anymore."

Okay, so this *was* the real Adolfo. What d'ya know?

And I did understand his fears. I'd spent at least a few thousand dollars on all of my classes, books, crystals, healing tools, oils, massage table, psychic readings, talking boards, oracle cards, bamboo beatings, and the list went on and on. I made a silent vow to make back all of the money I spent so far on my spiritual adventures by giving healing sessions. It was important for me to be seen as legit, a serious healer and not some woo-woo middle-aged woman going through a post-menopausal crisis, spending money like water.

Yet despite all that, Adolfo seemed to finally accept my dream of becoming a healer. Adolfo loved my YouTube video interviews. He liked to sit at my desk and watch while I stood behind him and gently caressed his shoulders and neck. "You are just as good as any newscaster on CNN or Fox News," he would say. "*And* you are prettier than any of those women." It hurts so much when he criticizes and belittles because he is often my strongest cheerleader.

My two interviews with Grace and Osairah had first pierced Adolfo's hostility toward my new direction. Talking to me on screen, Grace's screen presence reveals her as a beautiful, articulate, intelligent woman who seems completely normal. Adolfo was still quite skeptical when he saw it, but enjoyed watching Grace channel because he liked the message. "*And*, she's easy on the eyes," he said with a smile.

He even said, "Forget the board. You should start channeling like Grace."

"Adolfo, I would love to channel like Grace, but one step at a time. My tool is the board for now. Maybe one day I will channel without it. That would be amazing."

Adolfo just had a hard time with the board, and I was okay with it, as long as he didn't make fun of me for it. He referred to it using the Spanish pronunciation of the word Ouija, *kwee-hah*, which always made me laugh. I made a point to do it in private out of respect. Heck, even my mom—bless her—wanted to believe in all of my new interests, but gave me a blank stare when I brought out my board—until the proof came. I was visiting her at her home in Seattle and noticed a couple of areas in the dining room where the floor had some soft spots and seemed a little sunken. We couldn't figure out why the floor might be sinking.

I decided to use my talking board to ask Murth if she knew what was wrong with the floor. She replied that there was a leak under the house and that it was pretty bad. I immediately put my ear to the floor, and I could hear water running. That was incredible, but then she had me completely flummoxed. Murth said that she could fix it. *But Murth,* I asked*, how can you fix it?* She didn't have a good answer for that one, so we called the plumber. Note to self: my guardian angel is a spiritual guide, not a handy man.

So, was there a line that I had to draw of what I would accept through the board and what I could not? It invoked such fear in people. Dealing with the non-physical world—whether from the perspective of the New Age mindset or from that of age-old religions—requires faith, of course. Unlike the results of scientific experiments, no two people receive events and concepts in exactly the same way. So, ultimately we have to make the choice of what to believe and what to dismiss as either irrelevant or even wrong-headed. I feel so deeply enriched, strengthened, empowered, and just plain happy from my spiritual experiences, that I simply cannot limit myself to the "provable" events of the strictly physical dimension.

Many of my fellow students at the Imagine Center are extremely powerful healers and shamans whom I observed as they received messages during the hands-on healings, connecting with guides and ancestors. I greatly admired their skills and felt at home in their presence, but none had ever mentioned using the board. Once I brought it up in class, and Tauheedah said that she did not use the board nor think it was a good idea. I have learned that even in the spiritual community, opinions on what is safe, effective and plausible vary from teacher, practitioner, and seeker.

Even though I couldn't hear my guides when giving a healing session, I was feeling quite adept with my tool, the planchette flying at top speed over the board as my angel friends cheerily chatted, assuring me that I was loved and watched over. Still, I wished that I had someone to talk to that also used the board. Someone that I could swap stories and experiences with and who totally understood what I was experiencing. Julie was the only person in my inner circle who could fulfill that role, yet, I wanted someone whose skills went beyond my own, and I was about to fill that need. When you stay open to opportunities from all directions, you maximize your resources.

I took a break one day from playing Cupid and logged onto my account on Gaiam TV—now simply Gaia. There, I accessed George Noory's show, *Beyond Belief*. His program is a terrific spiritual resource, but part of the reason I tuned in so often was because I had been a guest on the show in 2013. They flew me out to Boulder, Colorado where the show was filmed, and George, a good friend of Adolfo, interviewed me about matchmaking, which was very generous of him, because his topics are usually on spiritual or paranormal themes. I worked the law of attraction angle, which is, of course, a mystical approach to dating. And I can say that some of the things I deal with in the matchmaking industry are definitely, *Beyond Belief!*

I declined the hotel room that was offered since I had a friend I could stay with, a smart, spicy, sexy, redhead originally from Texas who was known to wear cowboy boots with an evening gown. This is a small digression here, but I want to mention Robin because she is the essence of someone who lives the kind of joyful life that makes her angels boogie and keeps the Buddha laughing. She lived in Niwot, just outside of Boulder. Robin's resale shop, called Rockin' Robin's, was *the* go-to spot for people seeking Halloween costumes, funky retro attire, or just something fabulous. Among my several purchases from her shop was a gorgeous black antique kimono with pink and ivory flowers splashed all over the back. Robin and I go back thirty years when we both worked at the same café across from Fran's dress shop. Robin waited tables by day and did stand-up comedy in local clubs at night, and I used to accompany her to her gigs. We had so much fun back then—even though our boss was the boyfriend that kicked me in the shins. Robin used to say to me in her southern accent, "Maaaarrr-lah, whaah [why] are you still with hee-emm???????" And I would reply, "Because I looooove him, Robin!" And she would ask with growing disbelief, "Whaah??????" I wish I would have listened to Robin, but hey, hormones, codependency and fear were running my love life back then.

I hadn't seen Robin in person for five years when the chance came to be on the show with George Noory in Colorado. Robin and I whooped it up for three days of reminiscing, dancing, dining, and even hula-hooping in front of her store.

Every time I watch George's fascinating guests, I relive a little of that trip to Colorado. So, I was remembering all that when I read the description that day of George's latest episode.

With tales of demonic possession and unwanted poltergeist activity, the popular mythology surrounding the Ouija board is ominous at best. However, when used properly, it can be an effective tool to communicate with benevolent spirits. Ouijaologist, Karen A. Dahlman explains the history of and safe use of Ouija boards in this interview.

A Ouijaologist? OH, HELL, YES! I watched with delight as Ms. Dahlman, an articulate, smart, gorgeous blonde (my male matchmaking clients would describe her as a 10) explained to a curious, yet apprehensive George, the history of the talking board and how it works.

She went on to say that the oldest board in her personal collection of eighteen boards is a William Fuld OUIJA Board from 1902. But her favorite is the Parker Brothers—circa 1973—board she received from Santa Claus that year. Eventually George asked the question most on people minds, *have you ever had an evil spirit come through the board?*

Karen explained that it isn't the board, but the energy and the life of the person using it that calls in entities and spirits, the board is neutral, just a piece of wood or cardboard. "I could write letters on this table right now and put the planchette down, and it would probably start to move. Do you want to try it George?" She teased. He shot her a not-on-your-life look.

I had to get in touch with this woman. I quickly found Karen's Facebook page and sent her a message. She responded the next day and was gracious enough to set up a Skype call with me. We chatted like old friends for over an hour, swapping stories and showing each other our boards. We also decided to exchange books; she sent me one of her three books *The Spirits Of Ouija: Four Decades Of Communi-cation,* a "Ouija Tell All" and a forty-year odyssey spent communicating with her spirit friends from the Great Beyond.

Karen explained that she was writing two more books, this time about animal communication. "The cats are telling their story," she said.

"My cat Jack is telling one story about how cats have feelings and to stop people from being cruel to cats (his words) and the other cat story is with the help of my aunt in Australia about her cat who died and reincarnated and all the while the cat spoke with me via the board about its plight before he died, in the in-between world, and then, as a reincarnated cat. It's an amazing story about how love transcends all."

I had never thought to try animal communication on my board. After we signed off of Skype, I asked Murth if she could talk to Macie. She said *yes.* Wow, I thought and asked Murth if Macie wanted to tell me anything. Murth said, *Macie says that you are a very good mom, and she appreciates everything you do for her.* My heart melted. Ever since I found Macie on a street corner, we have been all but inseparable. I can't even go to the bathroom without her following me. She even knows how to do Facetime when I am out of town. As soon as she hears the specific ring when Adolfo calls me, she starts to howl, and runs over to look at me in the camera.

Becoming friends with Karen let me know that what I am experiencing is real. It's hard to explain, but there's a special bond there, sisters of a secret society of sorts. Not only has Karen been there for me in support of my use with the board, but she introduced me to some other incredible women who use the board as well. World famous psychic, Linda Salvin, uses the board to bring through several guides, including a well-known deceased musician who is incredibly accurate. He has a very powerful energy that comes through but has requested that his former human identity remain anonymous to the public. Linda only lives a few miles from me, and we will often get together for lunch at our favorite Mexican restaurant and then back to her place to chat with the musician. Some incredible messages and insights have come through, bringing hope, excitement, and clarity to current situations. One time when Linda and I placed our hands on the planchette, it moved with unusual force and spelled, *Marla get damn focused on your writing.* Whoa…I had never had such a clear message as that one.

The other dynamic woman I spoke with is also named Linda. Linda Deir was physically and emotionally abused at the hand of her mother from the time she was an infant. To be able to survive, her spirit guides came to raise her to adulthood. It all started with the "merry-go-round" dream that never changed; the first memory she had in this lifetime and one that she dreamed multiple times per night for the first thirty-five years of her life. From this single repetitive dream, her *spirit guide angels* made it painfully clear what her job was to be in this lifetime. It was to show others how to overcome their fears, so they too could live the life they intended before they came here—meaning before they were born.

I had the pleasure of meeting Linda and her husband Ray over Skype, and I also interviewed Linda for my show. They showed me how they used a special talking board that her spirit guides asked her to develop, that can be used with a pendulum or a small planchette. It's a great board to travel with. Linda even captured an incredible photo of her guardian angel, and put it on the cover of her book, *Guided.*

Karen and I started doing a video series, "The Women of Ouija," for my YouTube Channel. We discuss all sorts of spiritual and paranormal topics as well as self-growth and development. "Don't waste your time writing to us to tell us that we might accidentally conjure evil spirits, and that we shouldn't use the board," we said in our first video. "You will never change our minds; our experiences have always been positive and loving."

I knew that we were on the right track when one day I was reading the comments from viewers on a video about creativity, and was so touched when I saw this one:

> *Marla Martenson, you guys have inspired me to find myself! I believe I'm at the beginning of my journey of spiritual growth, but I am learning so much from you both. Thanks for your videos!*

Master healer, Deborah King, does caution that lower energies *do* exist, however, and these spirits, like humans, do not always have the best intentions. One hot summer night I was at The Imagine Center for healing team service. I'd silently endured a stomachache that evening with sharp pains and bloating, and was grateful when the sessions ended. I walked out from the back room and into the tiny retail where a young woman stood near the front desk. Sonia. I recognized her from my crystal healing classes. Slender and tall, dressed in black, she had streaked her long dark hair with purple and let it fall over her shoulders. Sonia seemed like a gifted healer with an intense, serious energy around her, but I had heard that she had been asked not to come back to the center.

Uneasy, I wondered what she could have done to be asked not to return. We greeted each other and exchanged pleasantries, but I noticed the healing team director, Susie, carefully observing us. Maxx, another gifted healer who also worked at the store, was burning sage, muttering under his breath and furiously writing something down on paper. I knew immediately that whatever he was doing had something to do with Sonia.

Sonia moved in just a few inches from my face as if to tell me a secret. "I see you are wearing your moldavite," she said, fondling the translucent green stone hanging from a chain around my neck. "Keep wearing it." Her eyes darted wildly up and down my body, as if she were deciding which section to take a bite out of first.

I could feel the energy shift to frenetic and funky, and I wanted to step away. However, my childhood conditioning had trained me not to give offense, and so I continued to let her invade my personal space.

She grabbed my left wrist and stroked the beautiful lapis stone on my bracelet with her thumb. Her wild eyes met mine again.

"Marla, how is your stomach?"

I was completely taken aback. How could she have known that I had a stomach ache? "Umm...well, it *has* been hurting all evening," I admitted. "How did you know?"

"I can feel it. I was called in here by Spirit tonight to give you a message."

"A message? For me?"

Sonia first placed her right palm on my solar plexus and then both hands on my shoulders. "You are adjusting to the energies of the new earth. You are upgrading, and your energy is expanding and your chakras are adjusting."

"Really? I thought maybe I needed to do a juice cleanse or something, or maybe I was constipated..." I said, attempting to lighten the mood.

She grabbed my wrist again and whispered, "I would like to teach you a few things…" She glanced down the hall in the direction of the healing room, eyes narrowing as she continued, "Things that you wouldn't learn here."

"Like what?" I asked.

"I'll be in touch," she said with a nod.

I told her that I needed to go pack up my things, and went back down the hall into the healing room. I felt oddly discombobulated.

All of a sudden, out of the corner of my eye, I saw Sonia fly down the hall and out the back door. She left so fast that it was like the special effects in the movies where vampires zip from place to place, transported in half a second.

Just as fast, Susie was standing in the doorway, hands gripped on either side as if to brace herself.

"Did she touch your crystals?" she blurted.

I put my hand to my throat, "Yes, as a matter of fact, she did. She was fondling my necklace *and* my bracelet. Oh, and she touched my solar plexus and shoulders too!"

"Maxx, get in here," Susie yelled, but in a stage whisper. "Sonia touched Marla's crystals."

Maxx scurried into the healing room. "She's dark. She's been getting into magic that she shouldn't be getting into. She's transferred the dark energy onto your crystals," he said, as he positioned himself in front of me, raised his left hand, and began swirling, apparently pulling the energy out of my crystals to cleanse them. Susie stood about a foot away, hands raised, stomping her feet to help break up the energy. Maxx worked diligently for a few minutes before he finished by smudging me with sage.

"You're all clear now," he assured me. I felt better. It was more psychological than anything, though. I liked knowing that my team had my back and made sure I was protected.

"She was not supposed to be here," said Susie. "I'm surprised she had the nerve to show up."

"Why is she not allowed to come anymore?" I asked.

"Because she was caught one day by Tauheedah, sitting outside in front of the store putting a curse on it," explained Maxx.

"Wow, that is unreal! Why would anyone do such a thing? This place is so positive and magical. I have never felt such amazing energy anywhere as in this space."

"Because, like I said, she's dark and dangerous," said Maxx. "But she won't be back. I'm sure of it. She knows that we know what she's up to."

"Maxx, what were you doing when Sonia was talking to me? Were you protecting the space or something?"

"Yes, and I was capturing her soul signature on paper. She was energetically not allowed to leave until it was captured. Once it was captured, she flew out of here!"

"And Maxx, what were you reciting over the paper?"

"I was reciting a mantra that carries a frequency to change the physiological system through shifting brain waves to clear a neurological pattern."

Besides being a healer himself, Maxx also works with frequencies, and he channels a Universal language of light with the permission of archangels and seraphim. I'm so open these days that I didn't roll my eyes at this when I first learned of this ability. And when I actually heard him speak it, a childhood memory came back to me.

My parents had become a bit concerned and wary when they heard me talking. I should have been asleep, but, as if in some weird Hollywood movie, I was sitting straight up, eyes open, staring straight ahead, and speaking in a language that they didn't recognize. Astonished, my mother turned to my dad and whispered, "Is our daughter possessed?" I guess it continued into young adulthood because I remember the boyfriend that kicked me in the shins telling me, "you talk in your sleep... some language that I have never heard before."

I asked Osairah about this in a group session one day, and they told me that it was most likely residue from a past life. They said I had a strong presence from Turkey, India, and Ireland. I thought it was pretty cool. Too bad we didn't have smart phones back then, someone could have recorded it.

Besides talking in my sleep, I was also a sleepwalker. Many a night my mother had to come and lead me back to bed after going into my brother's room, turning on the light and rummaging through his toy box, or wandering into the basement. The most embarrassing incident was when I spent the night at my girlfriend Lisa's house. I got out of Lisa's bed and walked into her parent's bedroom, stood over her dad as he lay sleeping, my long hair dangling in his face, and started talking to him. He must have thought I was insane.

Lisa's mother got up and led me back to bed. Once back in bed and under the covers, I remember thinking, *oh my God, what have I done?* But when morning came, I had forgotten about it. The next time I was invited for a sleep over, at the dinner table, Lisa's little brother Timmy warned his parents, "be sure and lock your doors tonight!" I was mortified. I had wondered if these unconscious experiences had anything to do with dark spirits or dark energy.

Driving home, I thought of how the energy of others is always affecting us, whether from a stranger or a family member. Deborah King calls it *getting slimed by negative energy*. It is important to shield ourselves energetically, so I usually wear a piece of black tourmaline around my neck for protection. I had forgotten to wear it that evening. Deborah says that if you're in a situation where you suspect someone may be sending negative energy your way, don't face that person head-on, but instead stand or sit at a ninety-degree angle so that you are at his or her side. This protects you from a direct hit of energy, whether intentional or not.

I would have to remember that if I ever found myself in another dark and uncomfortable situation. When I got home, I decided to ask Murth her take on lower or dark energy.

> *Rest assured, there is dark energy, but love will always prevail. God is love, and you are a spark of God. Very important to remember that all of us are divine. If a person goes off the path for a time and seems dark, be sure in the end that love will prevail. This message is read by many people and is very important. The only person truly dark is Satan, which is in the mind of man. People want to believe in a force of evil but man is trying to justify a dark side by questioning his own faith in the universe, and that is all it is. Try to believe in God's love, righteous love, and you will be just fine. Many blessings to you.*

Anything else, Murth?
Not now. You are loved. xoxo

I loved this message, and that she had picked up my use of *xoxo*. I also loved it that she'd revealed a certain independence from me with her message of "not now"—yet another proof that this wasn't just some aspect of my unconscious self that was having a conversation with the conscious *me*. Murth is truly a separate entity.

Experiencing profoundly meaningful communication with non-physical entities can cause me and others in this position to occasionally question and second-guess the "reality" of these encounters, especially if a loved one tells you that you are insane or dangerous. My otherworldly communications represent a state of grace for me. A lightness of being. They have impacted my life like nothing else, yet the process demands constant faith. Having three women in my life who are highly educated, articulate, dynamic, and successful, and who use a talking board, just sealed it for me. They were clearly not nuts. And I was NOT a loony-toon.

And th-th-th-that's not all, folks...

16

The Spirit Comes Over You and You Laugh

"You must enshrine in your hearts the spiritual urge towards light and love, Wisdom and Bliss!" ~ Shirdi Sai Baba

I love the idiomatic image of dipping a toe experimentally in uncertain waters, an act of both caution and courage. I picture a natural pool in a glen, rumored by some to be a fountain of youth and health, by others, a sorcerer's cauldron. Vapors rise from its mysterious depths, yet fireflies dance around a pristine white lotus, reflected on its ethereal surface. Is it a hoax to lure fools? Is it a mirage? Is it toxic? Is it magic? Can everyone see it or just me? What if it's magnificent? I summon my courage and dip my toe in, and a whole new experience takes place. I'm using this image as a metaphor, of course, for the invisible and mysterious healing energies I am learning to work with.

Besides doing talking board readings for Julie or with experts Karen and Linda, I had dipped my toe into the waters of mystical healing and was now in up to my knees, performing Reiki and crystal healing sessions and then offering angel readings—but only at the end of the session *if* the client wanted one. I'd acquired a few private clients, working in my office/sanctuary, which accommodated my massage table perfectly along with all of my magical tools and crystals. Kylie, an attractive strawberry blonde who was also in my database to be matched, had just been here. A regular, she came in twice per month for healing sessions with follow-up readings.

"This is so freaking amazing," she said today. "I wish I could come every day! The energy that comes through is so powerful."

Her guardian angel, who referred to himself as "Bob," gave her a message through my board. He assured her that love was right around the corner, but that she needed to first nurture the relationship with herself. *You are your best friend,* Bob spelled out, *so love yourself.*

This message held special relevance for Kylie, and she was so pleased with the session, she purchased a few more as gifts for her girlfriends—which is the nicest form of validation I could imagine. I was actually helping people.

So, back to the pool. The mysterious energies have become more than real. I see them as underlying everything. The more I learn, the more I want to know, especially, to what extent the world's spiritual practices relate to this energy. I came across the idea that in Japanese, the word *Reiki* comes from the character for *rei*, which carries meanings of a universal wind, spirit, or ghost. Reiki's creator, Dr. Usui, added *ki*, which is also known as *qi* or *chi*. The *ki/qi/chi* is that part of this energy that specifically sustains life, making the blend of energies the highest expression of that

which is universally sacred. *Ki/qi/chi* is a concept compara-
ble to the *ankh* in ancient Egypt. So the understanding of
this universal energy has been around a long time.

I'd come across the theory that Jesus had used Reiki.
This idea deeply resonates with me. The New Testament
mentions the many miraculous healings Jesus performed,
which included the laying on of hands, as Luke 4:40 states:

> *When the Sun was setting, the people brought to*
> *Jesus all who had various kinds of sickness, and*
> *laying his hand on each one, he healed them.*

He healed them whether they believed in him or not.
Just as Reiki doesn't require faith on the part of those receiving healings, Jesus lay his hands on sick people described in Mark 6:5-6 as lacking faith, yet "Jesus was still
able to use laying on of hands to heal." Disciples marveled
that he used a power that didn't deplete himself, which is
the essence of Reiki as well.

Another significant similarity Jesus' healings shares
with Reiki is the fact that Jesus was able to pass on the
power to heal to others, which is similar to the Reiki process
of attunement. The writings attributed to Luke clearly describe Jesus giving his twelve disciples power to drive out all
demons and to cure diseases.

Jesus imparted the power to heal to his disciples
through secret teachings as detailed in Matthew 13:10-11
and Mark 4:10-12 and 34. Similarly, Reiki symbols and the
process of attunements involve knowledge that are tradi-
tionally kept secret and only made available to those who
study with a Reiki master.

I wondered whether Jesus was born with the ability to
heal through touch or if this was something he acquired. His

activities between age twelve and thirty aren't mentioned in the Bible. Some researchers cite evidence that during these eighteen years, Jesus traveled to the East where he was schooled in mystical teachings from India, Tibet, and China.

Then I read a book, *Jesus, My Autobiography*, which was channeled through a woman in Canada, Tina Louise Spalding, who believed she had contacted Jesus. After reading the book, I also believe it. In her telling, Jesus recounts his life traveling to India and Tibet and learning healing modalities.

> *For the time that I was there, I studied with many you might consider to be gurus who meditated for extensive periods, practiced yoga, and these sorts of Eastern practices that are calming in nature and illuminating in energies.*

Jesus says that he was always connected to Spirit and non-physical entities and spoke of his healing abilities.

> *It became very apparent that my abilities in healing were magnificent and that I had been bestowed with this vision, an ability to see sicknesses within bodies and to see what was causing it.*

This book answered and substantiated my doubts about how the church and society have incorrectly taught about Jesus and His teachings. Jesus talks about the truth of his birth and the truth of his life. He covers some stories that are recounted in the Bible and tells us the true story of those events. He also describes some of his personal traits, human traits, and defines what he is, who he is, and why these things happened. He says:

You will be able to understand the truth, and you will begin this reconditioning, this retooling of your mind—of your thoughts and beliefs—on this subject of my life, my meaning, and my purpose.

I was thrilled to find this important book, which I feel in my bones to be truth.

As I worked with energy forces, they were at work within and around me. I loved how Kylie and others brought my healing work and matchmaking together. My cranky client, Brad, had been on his best behavior, and one day he sent me a sweet text, thanking me for his latest match. "I want you to know that I appreciate all that you do," he said.

Wow.

Miraculous shifts were occurring so powerfully they felt seismic. The best new development came in the form of a well-adjusted new client named Markus. In his late thirties, Markus was tall and lean with quirky good looks and a contagious laugh.

"I'm seeking a spiritual girl," he told me as we sat on his terrace overlooking the ocean, sipping lavender kombucha and munching on kale chips.

"I'm not interested in the typical materialistic Hollywood type. I meditate every day, and I'm lucky enough that my home-based business allows me to be in the ocean daily on my paddle-board with the dolphins. So, I want a girl that loves the water as much as I do."

This would be a delight. "Anything else?"

"Yes. I lead a vegan lifestyle, and it would be a bonus if she were also vegan or open to becoming one."

Ding-ding-ding-ding...My brain felt like a pinball machine, I had so many ideas bopping around in my head. I knew many beautiful yogini's in Southern California that loved the sun and the sand. Quite a few were vegan and would be a great fit for Markus. Vegans tended to be a tough sell to my male clients who hoped to meet a woman that enjoyed biting into a juicy steak and baked potato with gusto, washing it down with a nice Cabernet while maintaining a size two bodkin to boot. I constantly had to explain to them that the reason the women over forty who still have a rockin' bod is largely because they are extremely careful what goes into their mouths. "These are the women that might be on a juice fast or a cleanse the weekend you want to go to that trendy steak house," I often had to point out.

I mentally high-fived myself as I emailed Markus his first match. One of the photos that Markus sent to me for his bio was of him doing a headstand on his paddle-board in the ocean. I matched him with a gal named Gloria who had the same pose in a photo of herself, only she was also doing the splits! With the help of my angels, I just might be able to steer my career in the direction I want, making heavenly matches for realistic, peaceful, spiritually awake clients.

When work went this smoothly, I found time to broaden my spiritual pursuits. Julie and I had made unique plans for the evening, but first came a thirty-minute phone session with a healer from Florida who went by Jimmy Mack. An acquaintance had told me about Jimmy and connected us through email. After looking at his website, I was immediately intrigued.

After decades of studying and practicing a variety of healing methods, Jimmy had a near death experience in an ICU in the hospital that changed his life forever.

He was shown things and told things by spirit that allowed him to access All That Is and bring the ethereal rain that can make a difference in a person's life.

Jimmy uses a healing technique where he goes into the Theta brain wave meditative state and co-creates the client's healing with God/Source/Higher Power. During a session, both the client and practitioner enter a state of Theta automatically where physical, emotional and mental issues can be transformed in an instant. Even physical ailments can be cleared and healed simply by changing our beliefs. When we access the healing code and utilize the language of spirit we can alter our beliefs and our holographic structural design.

Whoa... alter our beliefs and our holographic structural design? I had to know more.

I'd already learned from Katt that distance healing can be just as effective as in person, so I was excited for the phone call.

Jimmy confirmed the belief. "Distance, time, and space are irrelevant, and it won't matter if I see you in person or over the phone or Skype. Spirit will still move in, around and through us to create profound and mystical changes in your life and mine."

He told me to think of a few things that I wanted to heal/clear, to wear comfortable clothing, be fully hydrated, and to have a pendulum handy. I knew immediately what I wanted Jimmy to work on.

"Jimmy, if you can heal this, you will truly be a miracle worker," I told him.

I hung up and did a fifteen-minute meditation with two candles burning along with a few dried leaves of sage, my beechwood pendulum within reach.

The phone rang promptly at 4:30. "Ok, Jimmy, this is the deal," I said in a hushed tone even though my office door was closed. Adolfo didn't know what I was doing.

"I love my husband deeply, and I know it's normal between couples to bicker to a certain extent. But the stress of his being on my case about the cleaning and organizing, and the critical aspect towards my spiritual interests can be so stressful at times that I fear one or both of us manifesting an illness or worse."

He murmured, listening, and I continued.

"One of the problems is that I tend to have knee-jerk reactions to his criticisms. If I could be in a state or non-reaction all the time, we might actually achieve harmony. After all, I need to look at why I have always attracted chaotic relationships."

My frustrations kept tumbling out, and I struggled against a spill of tears.

"We can both be hardheaded and stubborn," I went on, "until the friction ignites like two rocks being rubbed together to spark into fire. I can't seem to get ahead of his onrushing anger. I try to slam on the brakes, but it's as if...I'm just leaving skid marks where a car goes off the rails. So, I try so hard not to react, and half the time I can be cool and let it slide off my back, but the other half..."

"Marla," Jimmy's voice soothed, "consciousness acts like a super computer, and if we can change the software, we can change our lives by tapping into the field of our hearts, our feelings, and beliefs. We can transcend all of the laws of lack and separation, thus shattering our paradigm of limitations," he said. "Ultimately, I am clearing you, but spirit can do wonderful things, and hopefully, he [Adolfo] will shift as well."

I understood that, and while still connected to Jimmy, I prayed that the spirits and angels would work through me to burn through any past life residue, allowing the tiny glowing embers to rise into the atmosphere, disappearing into the void.

Jimmy's healing technique is called My Liquid Fish, which refers to a healing energy/thought flow that forms a fish-like pattern. Jimmy can work with the body or a pendulum. Working with the body, as I did then, you stand facing due north. After praying about what you want to clear, you say it aloud—for example, I am a procrastinator. If your body pulls you forward, that means yes, you are. Then Jimmy will perform his energetic magic with his guides—it just takes seconds—and then you say it again, and your body will be pulled backwards if the issue is clear.

If the client wants to use a pendulum, it works in a similar way. You need to have pre-programmed your pendulum ahead of time to know which direction indicates *yes*, and which direction indicates *no*. Hold up your pendulum, and make a statement, for example, "I am clear and moving forward." If the pendulum swings in the NO direction, then you are not clear, and Jimmy will do his thing, actually making the pendulum go in the opposite direction, indicating that you are now clear.

I did both that day, body and pendulum. Jimmy cleared the issue with Adolfo within seconds. I actually moved backwards, as if subtly drawn. I also asked to be cleared of my resentment towards my unrealistic/demanding clients and, lastly, of my procrastination in writing. I thanked Jimmy and promised to keep in touch. I'd kept a completely open mind and was hopeful, but remained skeptical that in ten seconds my marriage could be saved. It would certainly be an easy scam, but it felt authentic, and I'd long since made a cosmic promise to remain open and try as many spiritual modalities as possible.

Staying open had proven to be as vital to the process of enlightenment as any other element, and Julie and I had plans to try something entirely new. She'd learned of a Hindu temple/healing center right in the San Fernando Valley, not far from our neighborhood. It held weekly *bhajans* with a description on the website that read, "We chant to Shiva, Mother, Krishna, Guru, and Ganesh every Thursday. No experience necessary... just an open heart."

Julie had forwarded me the info to see if I wanted to go, so I looked up the definition and found that the term *bhajan* is used in India to refer to any devotional song, similar to the word *hymn*. Bhajans are sung all across India to praise God and express one's deep love and devotion towards the almighty. They are gentle, melodious songs that provide peace and wellbeing to both those who sing and those who listen to them.

Why not give it a try?

Julie answered the door at 5:30 that evening and told me to help myself to some fruit in the kitchen; she was just finishing up a business call with a new author. A bunch of grapes in hand, I settled on the living room sofa. Romeo emerged from the bedroom and took a defiant stance in the middle of the room, top lip curled back exposing his tiny set of rice-like teeth.

I was not intimidated. "Romeo, I have had about enough of this. I think it's time for us to be friends. You're behaving like a grumpy old man. I've been reading a book called *Past Lives, Present Miracles* by Denise Linn. Maybe you've heard of it. No? Well, I've come to the conclusion that you were a crabby old man in your past life, and you're not at all happy about being a puny Chihuahua in this in-carnation. Am I right?"

Romeo astonished me by jumping up on the couch next to me. He looked deeply into my eyes as if to say, *Si, señora, you got that right! I am pissed off! Some joke the Universe is playing on me. I guess because I was an asshole last time around, now I have to live as this sad excuse for a dog!*

"Romeo, it's okay. You can be as mean and nasty to me as long as you like, I will still love you." I risked getting nipped but dared to pick him up and held him to my breast. Then...I kissed the top of his head. AND HE LET ME!

Julie emerged from her bedroom at that same moment, jaw dropping. "Whaa—???"

"I told you I would win him over one day."

"Okaaay... I ...well, I am just in shock, Marla!"

Feeling like I'd conquered the world, I gave Romeo one last mushy kiss before setting him back down. "Goodbye, my little Romeo, I'll be back soon." It may have been my imagination, but I thought I saw him smile.

As we rounded the corner onto Ventura Blvd., I turned to Julie. "Do you realize that it's been two years now since we took our first class at The Imagine Center?"

"Oh yes, I do. I know exactly when it was, because that's when this WHOLE thing started with my neighbor. God, Marla, I wish I could just get over him. What is wrong with me? I mean how pathetic is it that I am still peering out of my blinds to make sure he is not in the front yard before I take Romeo out for a walk."

Evidently her candle exorcism of Sergio hadn't been permanent. "You don't want to run into him?" I asked.

"God, no. I mean, it's just too awkward."

I had trouble wrapping my head around the fact that Sergio treated Julie like a booty call and nothing else, toying with her emotions by texting her every few months in between girlfriends. She'd be accepting the idea of peacefully coexisting across the street from him, and then he'd contact her. I think she'd still drop everything and run over there into his arms if he even hinted that he desired such a thing. She deserved better. Julie is an amazing, intelligent, funny, and talented woman, usually strong in her convictions and opinions, but when it came to Sergio, she was reduced to a gooey pudding, unsure whether she was coming or going.

With Siri in charge of navigation, we arrived at the Tarzana destination in ten minutes—a residential neighborhood. Rolling along at the speed of a snail, I struggled to find the address in the dark. "I sure don't see any temple."

"Don't tell me the 'temple' is really a *house!*" Julie said.

"Look, you can see twinkle lights at the end of that driveway. That's the right address. Yep, it's a house, alright."

Julie sagged a bit, but I parked and reminded her that we were out for the adventure, trying something new. "And after all, it's only for an hour-and-a-half; we can handle that."

Glad that I wore a cozy sweater on that cold November evening, I walked with Julie down the long driveway. The *temple* was set up in a garage, carpeted and adorned with altars, statues, paintings of various saints, and candles, transforming it into a Hindu shrine.

We stopped at a sign posted on the wall outside. Women were informed that if they happened to be on their period, they should please sit outside in the driveway whilst partaking in the *bhajan.*

SERIOUSLY?

Julie and I gave each other a look that conveyed our mutual assessment: *this is fucked up.*

We seemed to be the first ones to arrive, and a whole-some-looking guy of about forty introduced himself as Ken and invited us to enter the garage/temple.

"Have a seat," he said, gesturing to the floor. He and his wife would be leading the *bhajan*, he explained, adding that they had lived in India for many years, becoming enamored with the Hindu faith. Julie and I selected a spot near the giant statue of Shirdi Sai Baba and sat cross-legged on the floor. "We also lead fire *pujas* once a week. You must come."

Julie and I were definitely interested in attending a fire *puja*, a ritualistic form of worship that has been used throughout the temples of India for thousands of years. The word *puja* comes from two Sanskrit words which together mean an act of purification of the mind, drawing in virtuous qualities while removing bad qualities or karma, essentially attracting positive energies and dissolving negativity.

Ken told us that Shirdi Sai Baba was one of the foremost *sadgurus* (a true guru) in India and lived in Shirdi, located in the state of Maharashtra, India for sixty years and elevated it to the status of a great spiritual center. It is said that though Shirdi Sai Baba is not alive in flesh and blood, he still lives and blesses his devotees wherever they may be. A large black and white framed photograph of the guru, sitting on the ground barefoot intrigued me. His hands, feet, and simple clothing looked filthy, a piece of cloth covered his head and tied in the back. His expression was serious and his eyes penetrating. The photo evoked someone who needed nothing, but had everything. I made a mental note to find out more about this guru.

A few other people finally arrived and took their places on the floor next to us. We chatted with a cute guy who was originally from Bulgaria and was a regular there.

"It's very powerful to chant and sing with other beautiful souls," he said. "I come every week."

Ken and his wife, Lida took their seats in front of us, and passed out some instruments along with sheet music with lyrics so that we could sing along. I chose a tambourine, and Julie selected maraca made out of a gourd. Ken and Lida started the *bhajan*, Ken on the guitar and Lida on the harmonium, a reed instrument with a sound similar to the accordion. I was surprised at how small the group was, only half a dozen of us. We all chanted and sang in Hindi.

Om Guru Om Guru

Paragpara guru omkara guru tavasharanam

Sukhakarshubakar hey parameshwara

Brahma paraparta vasharanam

Om Guru Om Guru

After an hour, Julie gave me the look. It clearly said, *okay, how much longer is this going to go on for?*

I glanced at my watch and whispered, "Should be only another half an hour."

We struggled on for another forty-five minutes as an Indian couple arrived, baby in tow, plates of food in hand. They placed the food at the feet of Shirdi Sai Baba and joined us in the chanting. Ten minutes later, three more Indian people arrived, bearing plates of food and placing them at the altar. Fifteen minutes later, four more with more food. Julie's stomach growled. We squirmed. My butt was sore, and I longed to stretch. I was not feeling the uplifting love I'd come for. Seated right smack in front of Ken and Lida, Julie and I had to communicate with our eyes, strained looks, and subtle nods. The place was lovely, as well as the people, but this was definitely not our thing.

I finally mouthed to Julie, "I can't take it anymore."

Julie stifled a laugh, and rolled her eyes.

Ken shot Julie a look of disapproval.

I felt like I was fourteen again and back in Miss Judy's dance class. My BFFs, Joni and Tracy, and I had smoked a joint in the parking lot before tap class and couldn't stop giggling as we shuffled off to Buffalo. All the while a frustrated Miss Judy shot scowls of disapproval.

The memory triggered a giggle, which also set Julie off. Uncontrollable laughter welled up, and we buried our faces in our hands, attempting to stifle the guffaws and giggles. Ken was glaring at us. Some people just don't get the Laughing Buddha.

I poked Julie in the side, "Come on, let's go!"

We jumped up and flew out the garage door like Aladdin on his magic carpet.

Still giggling as we sped away towards Ventura Blvd., Julie turned to me, her face flushed. "Okay, Marla, that was painful."

One more round of laughter burst forth, completely uncensored this time.

"It was truly not our thing, but I really want to go to the fire *puja*."

"Are you kidding? We can never show our faces over there again."

"I suppose not."

And yet it had proven an excellent modality—the laughter, actually; the meeting, not so much. I felt spiritually juiced, happy, and terrific. I like to think our angels and guides were enjoying themselves with us as well. That *bhajan* was the epitome of the confusion of spirituality with serious disciplined self-control—even though we were sitting on the floor shaking gourds and singing what to us were mostly nonsense syllables. There should have been all kinds of laughter and light-heartedness at that session. The Buddha loves to laugh.

Lighten up, world. Follow your hilarity.

Fear Nothing

"You are a ghost driving a meat-covered skeleton, made from star-dust, riding a rock floating through space. Fear nothing."
~ *Anonymous*

The morning after the *bhajan*, I sipped my herb tea on the patio off our bedroom. Beautiful sunlit swaths of magenta bougainvillea cascaded over the brick wall that separated our yard from our next-door neighbor's, yet I was less than blissed-out, worried I was looking for enlightenment in all the wrong places. For many, last night's gathering had been a portal or modality, connecting the soul to the greater universe, but it had devolved into silliness for Julie and me.

And all the psychics and channelers? Jimmy Mack had promised radical shifts that would produce significant changes. So far, well, yes, some good things were happening. I had gotten up at 7:30 to write. That counts as a quiet little miracle. (I romanticized my late mornings with a line by Christopher Poindexter, *I will never be a morning person, for the moon and I are much too in love.*) Yet the writing had put me in a thoughtful mood over recent events that weren't quite up to the level of what had been predicted.

Adolfo still rolled his eyes over my epiphanies and freaked out over trivialities. Last week I dropped a shoe on the floor, and he delivered an angry lecture. A scratch on a piece of furniture, a knickknack out of place, a clogged toilet, the loose faucet handle, even toilet paper hanging down *on the "wrong" side of the holder* could send him into a meltdown. His steady nitpicking and micro-managing often pushed me to the brink of my own melt down. The Virgo in him constantly demands perfection, while the Gemini in me wants to catch a ride on the next fluffy cumulonimbus, leaving the cleaning and organizing for later.

And I'd hoped to be able to cut way back on my matchmaking and eliminate the clients that seemed negative and difficult. If I were working more with energy healing and channeling, I could do just that. I'd tried my best, meditated, and prayed, yet I worried I might have reached a plateau. What if I'd already achieved my highest spiritual potential?

Little birds fluttered within the bougainvillea and chirped energetically in anticipation of a refill of sunflower seeds into the ceramic green dish that sat on a twenty-year-old, weather-beaten, wooden bistro table, bought during my single days in Chicago. Was I that much happier now than I was then? I'd created a sanctuary in my 400 square foot studio apartment located in the trendy River North neighborhood, right off Michigan Avenue. Along with the bistro table, I'd bought a York pie cabinet, a wrought iron room divider with a canvas screen, some glassware, and candles in Old Town. My little haven became my symbol of freedom from the verbal abuse of my ex-husband. Once Daphne—my teacup Yorkshire terrier—and I settled into the cozy little artist's loft, my fear of being alone melted away along with the icicles that were hanging from the eaves outside my window. Learning I could make it just fine on my own had felt very empowering and gave me confidence. It seems like the more you grow, the more you can see what lies just beyond. And then you want that too.

The little birdies twittered their impatience. I poured sunflower seeds for them and corn kernels and peanuts in the shell for the bushy-tailed squirrel I'd named *Sasha*. She arrived without fail every morning for breakfast. Recently, she'd included her two skittish young ones in her morning rounds. Macie paced back and forth in anticipation, but they kept their distance. A beautiful blue jay perched on a branch and cocked his head curiously. I smiled at his interrogative stance. *You got a problem, lady?* he was no doubt asking. *The sky's a dazzling blue and so am I, and my comrades are serenading you. Just count your blessings and gimme some peanuts already!*

Of course. I left another handful. He was right. I had a great life, and even though last night's *bhajan* didn't deliver, Julie and I had laughed our marbles loose. She was always up for an adventure, that was for sure, and we'd shared some doozies. I was so blessed that I had found such camaraderie.

Back in the house, I set about taking out the trash, but as I lifted the cumbersome metal lid, Adolfo walked into the kitchen. I lost my grip, and the lid went crashing to the floor. I winced and braced myself for the inevitable "*Aye, Marlita, be careful! You can damage the floor! Watch what you are doing. You are so rough with things.*"

But on that post-*bhajan* morning of the blue skies and blue jay and bougainvillea, a small miracle took place.

"That's okay, honey," Adolfo said pleasantly. "Don't worry about it."

Huh?

I scanned the kitchen. Yes, I was in the right house.

"Here let me help you," he said with a smile, lifting out the trash, and then grabbing a plastic trash-liner out of the closet and inserting it into the can.

This was BIG!

Dazed, I took out the trash and came back into the kitchen. Adolfo wrapped his arms around me and planted a tender kiss on my lips.

"This is a fresh start for us. I love you, Marlita."

I froze. A fresh start? Where was *this* coming from?

Then I realized...OMG. Jimmy Mack. He'd shifted Adolfo's energy, removing his fears...It had to be Jimmy, there was no other explanation for such a stunning reversal.

"I love you too, honey." Another kiss.

I had to get my head around this. When Adolfo went back into his studio, I grabbed my phone and Macie's leash, sending my little fur baby into fits of joy. Once outside and around the corner, I called Julie and told her the whole story.

"*Adolfo* said not to worry about that metal trash can lid *crashing* onto his beloved hardwood floor? That *is* a miracle!" She giggled.

"I know. I'm still in shock."

"I'll have to give Jimmy a try."

"He must be the real deal. And...*get* this: I asked Jimmy to work his magic on my habitual procrastination in writing my new book, and guess what? I was up this morning at 7:30 AM and got a whole chapter done. I *never* get up at 7:30. For anything. Let alone the brain challenge of writing."

"Maybe Jimmy can help me with my neighbor—speaking of which, I do have some good news. I signed up for a spiritual AA type of meeting. There's one every Wednesday night about a mile from my house. I figured it couldn't hurt to check it out. I'm pretty excited about it."

Hallelujah! Forces were at work, miracles were in the mix, and I could almost hear our angels applauding. Still on a high from the results of Jimmy's magic, I opened my computer and read an email from my client Kent.

> Hi Marla, unfortunately it's not going to work out with Kendra. We were having a great time at dinner, but then the conversation turned to spiritual matters. She told me that she is a Wiccan. The last thing I need is to date another nut case. Please find me a normal gal.

I knew an explanation about Wicca would not change Kent's mind, so with a sigh, I shot back an email, telling him I would be in touch with another match soon. A few years prior I might have had the same reaction as Kent if a prospective date told me that he was a warlock. I might have thought he possibly had a few screws that needed tightening, and would have sent him on his way.

Yet such preconceptions tend to limit experiences and relationships that might otherwise have proven enriching and satisfying. This fear of the unknown and the non-mainstream cripples the soul, clips the very wings that send it soaring.

On my spiritual journey, I have found it interesting that many people have a preconceived idea in their minds about matters of the occult, spirituality, and other unorthodox soul-related experiences such as Ouija Boards—as mentioned previously. I've encountered much fear-based judgment regarding Wicca, individual witches, and covens. The universal image of a witch conjures an image of an old, ugly, hook-nosed woman, casting spells while stirring her bubbling cauldron with her black cat—her domestic—hissing at her side.

Even with all that negative imagery of female witches, however, I admit I've always loved them. Halloween has always been my favorite holiday. When I was about ten, two girls in my neighborhood formed a "witch club" with me. My witch name was Hildegarde. I made up potions and wrote poems about witches. I've always believed in magic; autumn is my favorite season; and I love black cats and everything pumpkin. I definitely felt that I was a witch/healer in several past lives, and possibly burned at the stake for it, as I described earlier in my sense of historical outrage over the treatment of women branded as witches.

I have witch/Wicca friends, but it wasn't until I befriended Joanna DeVoe and Brenda Crozier, who live amazing, magical, beautiful lives, that I began to seriously pursue research about witches and their ideas. I discovered Joanna to be a woman who lives up to her self-description as a "kickass witch." She believes in the transformative power of love, the alchemical process of forgiveness, and the "Magick" of setting and holding an intention in order to manifest the *kickass* life of your most cherished dreams. She believes it's never too late to be the person you hoped to be. Joanna believes in rock and roll, meditation, daily exercise, green organic vegetables, nature walks, a great book, and a hot cup of tea—in other words, a great soul mate for me and many self-actualizing people. If that's what a witch is, then I am proud to wear the hat.

Brenda Crozier is a solitary witch in New England who is very passionate about her craft. She and I made heartfelt YouTube videos about everything from "wildcrafting," to Ouija Boards, space clearing, and spirit communication. She is a Reiki master and herbologist, and one of the nicest people I know.

Contrary to popular stereotypes, Wiccans are not devil worshippers, and, in fact, do not even believe in the devil. They do no animal sacrifices, nor any evil spells or deeds. Witches believe that the Divine is present in nature and that nature should be honored and respected. Many practicing Wiccans are passionate about the environment. I also love their celebration of holidays based on the turning of the earth and the cycle of the seasons. Today's homeopathic healers are the same kind of folk who would have been feared as witches back in the day.

Did hideous, child-eating old crones ever exist? Before modern medicine, the ramifications of falling ill or hurting oneself were gravely serious. Crones, a term that originally meant *wise woman*, were healers who understood the medicinal value of herbs—the basis of today's homeopathic treatments. Many sufferers turned to them for cures and for assistance in the delivery of babies.

As Christianity spread a powerful religious hierarchy across Europe, it also promoted patriarchal leadership and dominance, denying women any power not controlled by the church. Many healers also had psychic and spiritual gifts, so those who were most talented posed a threat to church dogma and its authority. Over time, the healers, especially women, were accused of heresy, being anti-Christian, and even of devil worship. Their craft was portrayed as evil sorcery, a part of pagan worship, and akin to black magic. Their assistance supposedly imperiled the immortal soul of a Christian, and people came to fear the very folk who could alleviate their pain and suffering.

If you are reading this, you too may have an inner *gnosis*, an intrinsic knowing deep in your marrow that a close connection to nature and the spiritual world are vital, so much so that achieving your highest, most authentic self evolves in this direction. Staying open to experience a wider, vaster realm than the boundaries imposed by most organized religions is the beginning of the journey to enlightenment. Light. *Lite.* Staying open means lightening up, expanding, laughing, feeling like Uncle Albert in *Mary Poppins* whose levity causes him to levitate! The laughing Buddha (*Bo Dai* or *Budai*) is thought to be an incarnation of Gautama Buddha from the future, though he is based on an actual tenth century Chinese monk. He represents contentment, generosity, wisdom, openness, abundance, and kindheartedness. He helps people realize the essence within, which connects with all beings. This path summons the opposite of condemnation, the opposite of fear.

I love this image and experience this joy often, especially since venturing into my spiritual journey, but there is much to distract me from such profound lightness of being. It is so easy to sink into fear and judgment. Looking forward to the joy of connecting with "my tribe," I opened Facebook. I have met and continue to meet some wonderful authors, healers, vegans, witches, Yogis and just plain awesome people there. I posted all of my videos on Facebook, and it was wonderful that so many people resonated with them and enjoyed what I had to share. I have had fun posting uplifting articles, photos, and ideas, and enjoyed reading others' posts greatly. While I love connecting with my peeps on FB, there is also the inevitable downside, which includes that pesky ego that we all have.

Someone brilliantly defined ego as *the sum of all our coping strategies for dealing with the bundle of our fears.* Our souls don't need egos, because souls aren't afraid. It is the "meat-covered skeleton" that needs the protection of an ego. Facebook is the ego on parade. Ageing beauties, fearful of independence, post scantily clad selfies, cleavage jutting out to the world in desperation, announcing, *hey everyone, look, I am still young and hot even though I'm pushing fifty. My implants, perky nips, pumped up lips, and hair extensions prove it right here in these photos.* And, of course, one can't escape the political rants, reflecting the fear of being dominated, the gloomy posts about depression and illness, reflecting pessimism, cynicism, and fear about the future.

Bragging is a form of ego-gratification, fortifying self in the eyes of the world—a pre-emptive weapon against fear. It can also be a statement proclaiming I have this and you don't. FB postings of photos of lovey-dovey couples, close-up shots of a hand with a big-ass engagement ring on it, or friends on exotic vacations can make us feel that they *always* lead happy, luxurious, exciting lifestyles. It seems that most of us can't help comparing someone's gain to our own lack and feeling like we come up short.

There is actually something called Facebook envy that suggests an addiction to FB can make you feel like everyone else has a better life than you do. The study has found that the more you use Facebook, the more the fear creeps into your subconscious, leaving you feeling deflated. I think Robert Sorokanich said it best in his article, "This Is Why You Shouldn't Take People's Facebook Lives Seriously":

> *Ultimately, Facebook is a narcissistic playground where the best, the funniest, the most charming aspects of our lives are publicized and the shitty stuff, the boring stuff, the beige that is most of our*

daily grind almost never gets posted. All those walls are edited at some level, and that makes them, at best, a deformed mirror image of real life or, at worst, nothing more than a fictional movie of how we want people to see us.

Having accumulated 3,000 "friends" on FB meant that I was bound to come across a trigger that pulled me out of my Laughing Buddha zone. A post from a distant family member showed up in my thread that upset me terribly. I was beginning to realize how unwise it was to keep so many people on my friend list, many of whom were total strangers. Adolfo had also reminded me that hackers could use Facebook to infect other computers with malware or a virus leading to identity theft. I knew I had some "unfriending" to do, but I put it off.

Being a vegan, I'm not at all keen on posts about how everything tastes better with bacon. I can usually brush that off, but as I was scrolling down my newsfeed, a devastating image caught my eye. One of my male cousins had posted a photo with the caption; "my brother went out for some fast food today."

The photograph captured said brother standing at the back of his pickup truck with a big smile on his face, rifle in hand, next to a dead deer. Other family members posted comments such as, "good job," and "awesome." I did realize that they have a different view on hunting than I do, yet as I looked at the doe's beautiful face and shiny black nose, I grew more upset. How could someone do this, let alone gloat over going out for fast food? I'd always felt great admiration for this cousin, but in that moment, anger, sadness, and despair filled me.

I heard a saying once and have never forgotten it: to every creature, his own life is dear. I do understand that predators, God's own creatures, must kill to survive, but most do it swiftly. Hunting/gathering humans like the African Bushmen still depend on meat, but they put their prey to sleep with a medicated dart, and then offer an apology to the animal for taking its life. A prayer of humble gratitude for its sacrifice followed. Modern humans, however, hunt more for sport and joke or brag about their kills, despite the fact that alternative nourishment is not only available, but that vegetarians are healthier than red-meat eaters, as mentioned earlier. I wish I could protect all of God's creatures from suffering. All animals are at risk, not only the deer in the woods, but also the beautiful sentient animals imprisoned in the factory farms, zoos, and circuses. Animals are exploited in dog fights and cock fights, the fur industry, medical experimentation, dog racing, horse racing, rodeos, bear baiting, bull fighting, and more.

Thinking of all that animals have suffered stoked the fires of my fears and anger, and I added my own sentiment to the Facebook feed: "DISGUSTING!" I promptly unfriended that side of the *whole fam damily.*

Was I hasty in my action? Some might think so. Adolfo expressed his concern about causing friction in the family. "I understand," I said, "but I cannot handle seeing images of murdered animals popping up in my news feed on Facebook." I recounted the story to my mom and shared how upset I was. Seemingly exasperated, she replied, "THEY EAT IT!" I shouldn't have mentioned it. She couldn't comprehend my anguish.

Not everyone is on the same path as I am on, but knowing that doesn't make the image of that lovely deer hurt me any less. It seems that sentient animals have every right to be here and have a life, just as much as any human.

I felt more and more confused, and I couldn't get the image of the doe out of my head. I've always been a sensitive person, but this horror reminded me just how much more sensitive I'd become since beginning my journey to enlightenment and feeling a deep interconnectedness to all of nature. Only one consciousness *would* understand my feelings and shed some light onto the subject, and she was just a thought away. I pulled out my board, breathed deeply, prayed my prayers for truth, love, and the light of guidance.

"Murth, you know how upset I am," I said, and asked my guardian angel for help.

As the planchette flew across the board, I stopped every couple of sentences to type what she wrote.

> *Yes, hello Marla. I want to say that you are a very loving human being. Rest assured that the undercurrent of human suffering is indeed caused by the violence to animals. A moment with a dog is very powerful, and could not be more beneficial to health. Not a day goes by without an animal suffering at the hand of man. So hard to accept, too hard to stand by and watch. Please know that man is responsible for the energy he brings. One day he will be called to answer for his abuse and cruelty. One day all will be revealed and the animals will be set free. Nature is a beautiful thing. An animal has every right to live in peace. A man that hunts a creature is a coward with a gun in his hand. Many animals don't have a chance.*
>
> *You are a sensitive soul Marla. Have patience, for God makes all things new. Love those for they know not what they do. Soon you will be in heaven with all of your beloved animals and*

many souls will see the light and make amends. Please forgive them as God does. Don't hate. Love is the answer. Can you please tell your readers that I love them all? They are all God's children. Many have gone astray but can change the direction of pain if they so choose. And please remember that many animals are here to teach us compassion and forgiveness and also love so strong it cannot be broken by people's ignorance that all life is sacred. Thank you for hearing my message, I am happy to be transmitting from the seventh dimension. And please do not hesitate to come to me for support for anything. I love you all.

I was awestruck. This felt spot on to me, and I pondered it for a bit. I was also curious what Murth had to say about living in the third dimension on planet earth as an ultra-sensitive soul such as myself.

Yes, Marla, I want to say that having an open mind to the transition of the world's energy shift begins to resonate with another earth. Please find a place in your heart for very loving energies that are trying to connect with the oneness of humanity. If you can do this one thing, all will be revealed; not as a virtual mandate but as a sane world in a chaotic time. Please be vigilant and question your capacity for compassion because we are in radical change and need a miracle soon. That miracle will come from inside each and every one of you so be prepared for radical changes in the universe as energy shifts to a higher frequency.

I'd heard other talk of the earth going through an energy shift, and in my private session with Osairah, they told me that I am a Blue Ray and that *the Blue Ray beings are an ultra-sensitive empathic soul group like the Indigos that came from many different ascended planets and light realms to enlighten the genetic code of humanity and raise the God-consciousness on mother earth.*

Animals were not the only ones to fear man, for the violence against humanity was showing up more and more frequently, it seemed. With terrorist attacks becoming more frequent, people are on edge and questioning their safety. Murth's message on terrorism:

> *Only one thing about that. People are scared and confused, understandably, but love will outweigh hate in the end, and when terrorists strike, it brings out the best in humanity to band together and unify so that all righteous humans can justify making a very safe and happy society, and God knows we angels are doing our best to make sure that women are in charge because the men have messed things up long enough. Please know that we love men and women, but things need to change soon or disaster is imminent.*

Whoa! Murth is even more of a feminist than I am! "Anything else, Murth?" I asked.

> *Not now. I love you all. Bless you.*
> *XOXO,*
> *Murth*

Marla Martenson

As always, I was grateful for Murth's insight, especially since I needed to convey my highest sensibilities in my interview with a very exciting guest on my show that day. I also needed to look my best for the camera.

As I got ready, I felt like I'd hit the big time, since I would be interviewing Paul Selig, writer, teacher, and medium. I had watched every YouTube interview I could find of Paul, because as far as channelers go, he offered a formidable level of credibility. Even Adolfo thought that Paul was super cool and enjoyed watching his videos. Of course I believed that Grace/Osairah, Ester Hicks/Abraham, and Darryl Anka/Bashar are all the real deal, but because Paul Selig is an academic, a professor, and a playwright who graduated from Yale and had been raised as basically an atheist, or agnostic at best, he'd had to surmount his natural skepticism in some way to become a channel. He says that he is not a "woo woo" guy. "I'm not a guru, I don't wear a turban, and the last thing I want to be called is a spiritual teacher. I am a student of this work as well. I am learning from the guides along with the reader."

Paul was raised on Manhattan's Upper West Side and had been taught that people who had a spiritual life, or believed in such things as psychics or mediums were deluded, ignorant, or, at least, not to be taken seriously. But then a spiritual experience, that he thinks was most likely a Kundalini awakening, occurred in 1987 on the rooftop of the building where he lived in Chelsea, enabling him to see little lights around people, like fireflies. He then studied a form of energy healing, and he found that when he placed his hands on his clients, he would hear messages for them.

Paul began to evolve more and more as a clairaudient and later a conscious channel. His guides, a consortium of beings from a higher level of consciousness, had arrived and were there to teach. In 2009, his guides announced, quite unexpectedly, that they had a book to write, and two days later, they began to dictate the text of *I Am the Word,* which they described as a treatise on the manifestation of Christ in man. They also stated that the book was an energy transmission that worked directly on its readers to bring them in accordance with the frequency of the Word, which they defined simply as "the energy of God in action." Many readers report that their whole body begins to vibrate while reading the book. Three more books were subsequently channeled through Paul, with more to come.

The interview went beautifully, and I looked forward to attending an in-person workshop that Paul and the guides would facilitate in Los Angeles soon. Discovering that so many non-physical guides, entities, and angels were starting to help me put my fear aside and trust in a higher purpose, I felt the energy shifting and prayed things would shift soon for humanity and the animals alike.

Over the next few weeks, I started to have powerful sensations at my crown chakra. I could feel the energy at the top of my head, as if someone was lightly touching my hair. I was excited because I figured it meant I was opening up more and possibly becoming more psychic. It had also happened on occasion in the middle of the night, a strange sensation that would zap through my brain; the sound was a sort of buzzing sound with a vvvzzzzzzzvvpp! One night it actually jolted my head off the pillow. I turned onto my side, and instantly, my body was filled with the most intense energy I have ever felt.

I had been asking for a high level guide to connect with me in order to channel. So, I assumed that the sensation in my brain was an entity trying to connect with me. The energy that took over my body felt as if an alien had entered through my crown chakra and had taken over. I was paralyzed for a few moments and I realized that my mouth was wide open as well, so I figured whoever was here was trying to speak. The energy felt dark and it frightened me terribly.

I mentally called for The Archangel Michael to come and stand in the room for protection, and then I told the entity to leave. The energy left right away, but my body remained tingly, and I was breathing heavily. Tears filled my eyes as I tried to comprehend what had occurred. I silently apologized to whoever had made a visit, just in case they were a high level guide just trying to make contact, the contact I had wanted for the past two years of my enlightenment journey.

On the way back from the bathroom, Adolfo heard my labored breathing.

"Are you okay?"

"Someone or something just entered my body, and I think I was starting to channel."

"You're losing your mind! Go back to sleep."

"Adolfo, I swear to God, my body was taken over, it was so powerful..."

"Uh huh... okay, honey, goodnight."

I finally got back to sleep, but the next morning I told Adolfo about my encounter in detail.

"Geez, I heard you breathing so heavy, I thought you were masturbating or something."

"Very funny! I am telling you, something really strange was happening. It was possibly a guide coming through to channel."

"Ok, honey, I do believe you." He looked at me thoughtfully. "This is pretty cool."

"Will you sit with me one day while I try to channel?"

"Sure, that would be cool if you started channeling for real. I'll help you."

You see how things were changing? I was still making spiritual progress of some kind, but I had more work to do on my fear of allowing another entity to channel through me

The Paranormal Couple and A Ghost Named Crystal

"I mean, you could claim that anything's real if the only basis for believing in it is that nobody's proved it doesn't exist!"
~ J.K. Rowling

I thought about the adventure that Julie and I had embarked upon that auspicious October eve when we took our first class at the Imagine Center. I was in awe of how much I had grown but also knew that I had a long way to go because enlightenment shines a powerful light into the dusty corners that still need to be swept clean. From the get-go, I knew that I had much work to do on my relationship with both Adolfo and myself. Clearing out old patterns of co-dependency, playing the victim, and playing small were the issues that I needed to tackle.

Through raising my vibration with energy healing, study, and self-reflection, I was able to finally get ahead of some of it, and I felt lighter and on a more accelerated track to the divine.

The saying goes, *you can only change yourself.* Abraham, a group of enlightened guides channeled through Esther Hicks, explains that those around you will then either shift as well—to resonate at the level of your vibration—or they will spin out of your energy field (out of your life).

I had prayed that Adolfo would shift rather than spin out, since I was not willing to water down my journey to make someone else feel comfortable, even my own family. Since the session with Jimmy, he was definitely spinning towards me, rather than away. We did not have even one major argument, and when nerves did occasionally get a bit agitated, we were able to correct ourselves within minutes and hop right back on the peace train.

I was especially astonished one day when Adolfo and I were in my office watching one of my videos that I had just edited. After it was over, I tentatively said, "Honey, would you like me to clear your energy field and check your chakras? It will only take a few minutes and you can just sit right here in your chair. I really think you'll like it."

Adolfo paused and then pointed to my massage table that was stored under my love seat, "Or, we can get out the table."

"You mean that you want the whole treatment?"

"Sure, why not? I see how people love your healings. Let's do it."

I pulled the table out from under the love seat and set it up as he took off his shoes. He climbed up onto the table and lay on his back. I placed a silk mask over his eyes and closed the blinds in my office. After clearing his energy field, I started giving him Reiki.

As I worked, I flashed on an incident a couple of weeks prior at the Imagine Center. I was on the healing team that night, and the other healer and I were chatting as we waited for our next client to pay at the front desk before she came back to the healing room. All of a sudden, my throat closed up. I could barely speak and was in terrible pain. I had no idea what was happening. When the client came into the room, she explained that she had an issue with her throat chakra and would like us to pay attention to that area. Interesting, I thought. I seemed to have taken on the physical symptom of the client. About ten minutes into the session, as I was giving her Reiki, I felt as if I had heartburn. Now, mind you, I have never had heartburn in my life. I asked the client if she had heartburn, and she affirmed, "Yes, I've been having heartburn lately." Then my feet started to hurt, and, sure enough, she also confirmed that she had been having pain on the bottom of her feet. I realized that this was empathic work. It was both exciting and strange. My skills were developing to a higher level.

When I got home, I did some investigating on the Internet and found out that empaths are the psychic sponges of the world, soaking up all the psychic and emotional static that other people give off. No wonder I was so hurt by the suffering of billions of animals. Being an empath is one of the most common yet most challenging of all the psychic gifts, which can be both a blessing... and a curse.

Adolfo seemed to be totally blissed out during the whole session. When I finished, I helped him sit up, and he swung his legs over the side of the table.

I was dying to hear his reaction. "Well, how do you feel? Did you like it?"

"I felt the energy; it was incredible. You *are* powerful. I feel amazing. Thank you, mi amor."

I swear I felt someone touch my left side, possibly Murth giving me a friendly jab in the ribs, as if to say, *I always knew, he would come around one day.*

Feeling especially confident now that he believed in my healing powers, I rushed into the kitchen and grabbed a juice out of the fridge. I handed him the glass of fresh carrot/apple juice and proceeded to share something that happened the day before.

"So honey, something incredible happened yesterday when I went over the hill for my dentist appointment. I mean *really* cool!"

Adolfo guzzled the juice. He, like Julie, isn't too keen on my green gunk but will drink carrot/apple since it's sweet. "Yeah?"

"Well, I thought since I don't go that way much, I would see if there were any cool metaphysical gift shops that I didn't know about, so I looked at Yelp and found one called Mostly Angels and Other Magical Things. The reviews were great, so I drove over."

"Marlita, I hope you didn't buy anything. You have so much stuff, you could open your own shop."

I decided against sharing my excitement about the elestial quartz crystal—that's *elestial* not *celestial*. It was a bargain at $65.00, so I bought it. I know, I know, I promised to be more responsible with my spending. This was the last one, I promise...but this one is *really* special. I was hoping it could help with opening my third eye.

My handy crystal guide says that elestials aid with attunement with the higher vibrations and open doorways to higher dimensions. They are an amazing stone that provides a stronger connection to spirit and to the angelic realms. The Divine beings, including angels in the higher realms, know what you require and these lovely crystals are an excellent conduit to bring in love and light, at the right time and in the right way for personal growth.

I told Adolfo how I walked into the tiny shop, a delightful elderly lady named Ruth greeted me as she sat behind a cluttered glass-topped desk. While chatting about crystals, I sat down across from her, and she opened her crystal guide to recommend her favorite crystals for protection and abundance. "She was so interesting, I could have sat and chatted with her all day."

"Uh-huh."

"Okay, the incredible part was that off to the left, behind Ruth, facing me, a pair of swinging, louvered saloon doors led to the storage room. They opened—all by themselves! Then a couple of minutes later, one of the doors closed, then opened back up again, and so on and so on."

Adolfo rolled his eyes. "Oh, that was probably a ghost. It couldn't possibly have just the wind."

"But there was no wind. That was the first thing I thought of too, but the front door was closed. I even got up and peeked through the saloon doors, and the back door was closed as well. And there were no fans in the place either. That's when I jokingly said to Ruth, 'Hey, do you have a ghost or something?' And she answered, 'Yes, honey, as a matter of fact we do. That's Crystal. She used to work next door. She died and has been hanging around here in my store. She likes to jingle the wind chimes and open and close the doors'."

"Okay, Marlita, now you're losing all credibility with me again. I was opened-minded with the Reiki and the crystal healings, but now you want me to believe there was a ghost in the store?"

"Adolfo, listen to me. I was flabbergasted. I've been waiting for an experience like this my whole life! I asked Ruth if it was okay to talk to Crystal. She said to go ahead. So I said, *Hello Crystal, nice to meet you. Would you mind opening the door again?* And Adolfo, she did! The door swung open!"

Adolfo was laughing now. "You are *so* gullible. It's a trick. The old lady has a button she pushes to open and close the door. Don't be ignorant!"

"No, she was *not* pushing a button. The desktop was made of glass. I saw her hands the whole time. There were no wires on the door."

"Then it's programmed. Maybe a foot pedal. I know about this because they do it in Mexico. And besides, Marlita, if there was really a ghost there, it would be all over the news, she would be famous! Honestly, there is nothing that you won't believe."

"Adolfo...I'm telling you...it was real! You can come over there with me if you want, and see for yourself."

His expression conveyed that wouldn't be happening. "Thanks for the healing treatment and the juice, mi amor." He laughed as he shook his head and retreated into his studio. "Aye, Marlita!"

I went onto Yelp and read every review about Ruth's store. Each one of them raved about what a sweetheart she was, and how much they loved her and the little shop. I found it odd that not one review mentioned Crystal, so if the door swings were some kind of stunt to attract the curious, someone would have mentioned it, and a controversy would reflect Adolfo's suspicions. I do understand his skepticism. Intelligent people consider all the angles. Yet a supernatural angle is one not to rule out categorically, in my opinion. Was I too gullible? Did I want to believe so badly that I could be duped easily?

I think there may be another side to being an "empath." I absorb other people's ideas, especially when it comes to the spirit world, and tend to lose my objectivity, like the time I became obsessed with looking at orbs through the camera on my Iphone. I learned of a technique from an older gentleman, Hank, who ate at the church where my mom helps feed the homeless on Friday nights. On one occasion, the usual crowd had gathered and helped themselves to franks and beans and potato salad. Aside from Large Marge complaining, "beans *again*," the people tended to be touchingly sweet, appreciative, and hopeful. My favorite guy, O'Brian, a tall, good looking Filipino, who seemed to wear all of his clothes at the same time, always had a "gift" for me when I visited—a pamphlet from a Korean church, a packet of top ramen, hard candy, a pack of gum or a Bible. Hank and his wife Connie finished their meal, and Mom introduced us. They weren't homeless, but their income was low, so to make ends meet, they often found hot meals at local churches. My mom fondly called them *the paranormal couple* and knew I'd want to meet them. Hank's camera had captured what he said were lots of spirits in the form of tiny orbs of light. I looked on with great interest as Hank showed me the video of several orbs gliding in an arc, hovering, or zooming around in the living room of his mobile home. His wife shrugged and visited elsewhere.

"She's not interested in the spirits," Hank said.

"She doesn't believe these are spirits?" I asked.

"Oh, yeah, but she doesn't see what difference it makes, even when they freak my cat out."

"Seriously? The cat sees them?"

"She sometimes jumps two feet in the air! The spirits get all agitated when I shine a light in that corner in the back," he explained as he pointed at the camera. "And I've felt them touch me, too. But otherwise, they really don't bother us."

Hank also told me that a paranormal investigative team had been out to their place and wanted to do some filming for a TV show. He showed me how to see orbs on my camera and encouraged me to try it at my house and see if I had any spirits lurking around. "Email me and let me know what you find."

So, one night in my office/sanctuary, I turned off all of the lights, and turned on the video (without pressing record) with the flash on. Looking through the screen, I immediately saw orbs flying around like crazy. Big, little, zooming by from all directions, not only side to side, but at times, shooting straight up seemingly coming out of the floor. I leapt with excitement. I pressed *record* and videoed my orbs to show Julie. I also watched, via the camera, a few of them fly around in the living room, and lots in the bedroom. So started my obsession. I would lie in bed every night, before Adolfo got home from work, with my camera on, watching the orbs dance around the room. Most were white, but some that sped by were green, pink, or yellow. Sometimes, an orb would fly slowly, zigzagging towards the camera and then stopping right in front of the lens before disappearing out of view. I was certain that these were angels or spirits. I showed Adolfo, thinking now I had concrete proof that spirits/angels were real!

"Marlita, don't be ridiculous, those are not angels, it's just dust, or a reflection from the camera. I've read about this on the Internet. I know about cameras and recording equipment. Believe me, you aren't seeing angels through your camera."

"But Adolfo, they're different colors, and sizes, and move at different speeds. How can it be dust or reflections? I don't get it."

He would just shake his head. "You're wasting your time looking at dust particles. I'm telling you, it's not angels."

So, I did some digging on YouTube and found a video that a woman made about these orbs. She said that it was just dust and to prove it, she shook a blanket on her bed and then started filming. Tons of "orbs" flew out. "It's just dust!" she said. I had to admit, the orbs that she filmed, looked exactly like the orbs on my camera. I guess the light hitting them formed little halos like the kind you see from the sun in daylight photography when the lens is pointed at or near the light source. With warm air constantly rising, and cold air falling, I guess subtle currents at different rates made the dust orbs rise and fall and swirl. As to the different colors, I figured it must be the reflection of light.

I felt like a total idiot. I even felt shame. I had told Adolfo, my mom, Julie, and several friends. I even showed them off on my camera. I was so disappointed that I stopped looking at my orbs for months. But I still wanted to believe. I thought that maybe both scenarios could be true. Maybe some of the orbs were real spirits.

Later, I was cleaning out my computer, deleting old photos, and came across three pictures that I'd taken in an old historic hotel in downtown Los Angeles. I had just left my job at "Double D Dating Service," and was trying to scrape up my share of earnings. This was before I'd started my own matchmaking service, and I landed a gig as an extra on a TV show. I played a cop, standing in the background at the precinct, which was recreated on the hotel's third floor. We finished shooting around 7:00 PM, and on my way out, I snapped a few photos in the lobby of the majestic old hotel to show Adolfo. He'd admire its ornate marble staircase and beautiful architecture. Looking at the photos, I noticed several orbs hovering on the staircase. I counted eight orbs in all and the largest appeared to have something in the middle. I enlarged the photo and saw what I interpreted as a tall angel in the center. The other orbs had rainbow circles inside. The photo opened my window of possible belief again, however, and it felt exciting. My belief surged again when I was watching one of my YouTube interviews and saw an orb fly across the screen. And then it happened again in another interview. They were obviously NOT reflections off of my camera.

A funny thing about belief, it feels so good. It stokes our optimism and shoots endorphins through our cells, helping them to operate at optimum performance. That's a good thing, a bargain in health care, both mentally and physically. We know that Santa and the Tooth Fairy aren't real, but it was such fun to believe while it lasted that we deliberately persuade children that they too should believe for a while. We can then vicariously re-experience that rush of joy and magic through their eyes. The let-down may be harsh, but then we find other things to believe in. We have to keep believing in something greater than ourselves, more dimensions, more possibilities. That openness to magic can strengthen us through the hard times.

Not long after seeing the old hotel photos, I'd met another energy worker named Misty at a healing event. We decided to trade healing sessions for each other, and I went to her apartment in Hollywood one evening. The mutual sessions were amazing, and before I left, we sat on her sofa, meditating by candlelight for a few minutes. She was highly spiritual, and her cozy place was absolutely magical, its gigantic crystals adorning shelves everywhere. A gorgeous statue of Mother Mary stood in the center of an indoor water fountain, bubbling away. Soft tribal music was playing as I told her about my orbs.

She looked at me, a slight amusement in her eyes. "Want to take a look?"

Indeed I did. She snuffed the candles, skootched over next to me, and we peered through her camera into the darkness. Several orbs flew by, and then an ectoplasmic entity the size of a toddler slowly drifted across the room. Now that was NOT dust or smoke or camera lens phenomena or a mutual hallucination.

Those who demand absolute proof may be right in specific instances, but their wet blanket doesn't provide much joy and comfort. It doesn't trigger the release of endorphins or other positive neuropeptides. I know there is a powerful Mystery that has created existence, that we're all tiny fragments of it, and that all the possible outward "signs" let us feel a moment of intense connection to it.

Me? I'm staying open to belief.

Donuts, Deceit and an Explosion

"Live in such a way that you would not be ashamed to sell your parrot to the town gossip." ~ Will Rogers

Adolfo was quiet and had a certain dreamy look in his eye as we enjoyed our usual Sunday breakfast at a local Mexican joint. I can usually read his expressions, but not that morning. He could be planning to say something like *I think we should move to Seattle or maybe Cozumel.* I felt as if I said the wrong thing, I might shatter something important, but the suspense was getting to me.

"Ya know," I said between bites of my vegan enchiladas with salsa verde, "I can't believe that in all of the San Fernando Valley, there is not one other place that has a good Mexican breakfast. I mean, are we going to be coming here for the rest of our lives?"

We chatted about restaurants. I'd also tried to convince Adolfo to try the Sunday brunch at my favorite vegan place in Studio City, but every Sunday for the past five years, we've been going to the same spot. It's as authentic as you get, and their salsas and homemade tortillas are perfection. Great coffee, too. But would a little variety kill him?

"Honey," he finally said, "I was thinking..."

"Yes?"

"Well, I think I'd like to get an angel reading."

"Adolfo, are you serious? You're pulling my leg. Right?"

"No, really, I'm serious. You told me Steffany is wonderful, and I really like her energy when I watch her on the videos with you."

My turn to remain silent. Maybe Adolfo was trying a new tactic. He pretends to go along with me, then says, *hey, I tried*, and scoffs anew.

"Look, Marlita, I hope I can see an angel one day, but even if I am not convinced, I'm just happy that you're happy and enjoying yourself. I want to believe in what you believe, and I want to try to be more understanding."

The heavens had opened up and harps strummed. This was awesome. Unless it was just a token gesture. "That's great..." I said uncertainly. "Just great..."

"So, can you set up a reading for me?"

"Sure," I said. My mix of awe and doubt didn't stop me from snagging the last tortilla.

After breakfast, Adolfo and I hit the mall. I needed some new bras since my B cup bras no longer fit properly—perhaps a few too many Sunday tortillas. We located the Victoria's Secret, and Gloria, the "bra specialist" helped me. I held my arms up and explained my weight gain. She measured me and announced my new D cup size.

"WHAT? Are you sure about that?"

She brought an array of black and nude bras that looked impossibly beyond my size, but they fit. Geez, my boobs had exploded! I'd have to tell the girls in my matchmaking database to skip the plastic surgeons and just wait for menopause.

I put my shirt on over a new bra and stepped out to show Adolfo, strutting ever so slightly to show off the new cleavage.

"Wow," he said with a meaningful look. "Guess I have angels too."

So, with angel energy suffusing our relationship, I booked a reading for Adolfo with Steffany when we got home. He had to play for a private party that night, so I invited Julie over for some girl time. It was an unusually warm autumn evening, so we headed outside.

"What happened to *you*?" she asked as she followed me out the back door. I flipped a switch, and the swimming pool lit up, a shimmering turquoise.

"Oh that...well, I guess I gained a little weight."

"Okay girl, why can't *I* just gain weight in one place? Well, two places. This is totally not fair."

I laughed as we sat at the patio table. Macie jumped up on the chair next to Julie. "So what's new? How is your spiritual anti-drinking meeting been going?"

"Well... it's okay. There are some pretty strange people that show up, but it's literally a few blocks from my house, so there's really no excuse not to go..."

I waited for the *and*.

"And I *have* been drinking *a lot* less..."

"Julie, that is awesome. I'm so proud of you! I know how much you love your margaritas." There was something she was deciding whether to reveal or not. "And...?"

"And there's another incentive to show up..." she said with a grin.

"Oh?"

"Yeah, well...there's a super sexy fireman who attends, and he doesn't drink at all, because he had a DUI. Anyway, we really hit it off, and after the meeting every week, we go to Dunkin' Donuts for coffee and conversation. He's so sweet, *and* he thinks I'm amazing."

"Julie, oh my gosh, well, you ARE amazing! This is fantastic news, now maybe you'll forget about that fuckwit, Sergio..."

"Yeah...not so fast...there is *one* little problem..."

"Oh nooooooo! Don't tell me..."

"Yup."

"Married????"

Macie shot her a look, then jumped off the chair and went into the house.

"JULIE! ANOTHER UNAVAILABLE GUY?"

"Okay, Marla, I know, it sounds bad... but he has a terrible marriage, and he's just staying with her because of the kids..."

I put my head in my hands. Was there ever a guy who cheated on his wife who didn't use that line?

"Marla, it's okay. Really. Nothing's happened. We just sit there and talk—granted, all googly-eyed—but, it's like we're in Jr. High or something, all very innocent. It makes me feel good. Something to look forward to, and we're just friends. Yes, there's a spark, but it's just donuts and coffee for goodness sake!"

"Julie, I just don't want to see you get hurt, that's all."

"Look, I took your advice last year and went out *three times* with that short, bald, Jewish accountant."

"Ohmigosh, I almost forgot about him. Stan, right?"

"Yes, poor Stan, he was trying so hard to impress me. Remember, he took me on that hayride at Christmas time? And he took me bowling at a place that served *the* best margaritas."

"Yes, I remember now. You see, Julie, Stan is the type of guy you should be with; a man who dotes on you and adores you. Why you didn't give him more of a chance?"

Julie gave me a dead-pan stare. "Marla, I guess you forgot."

"What happened?"

"The last straw was when he dipped his fry in my ketchup."

"So?"

"I have a thing about that. *Do not be all up in my food, and in my plate.*"

I had to laugh. "Wow. The French fry that shot down a bright future." I considered for a nanosecond knocking on Sergio's door and offering him a hundred bucks to take Julie out for a burger and then dip a fry in her ketchup. "Okay, well, let's hope the fireman doesn't dunk his donut in your coffee!"

"Ha! Very funny. Okay, enough about me, what's happening with you?"

"Oh...major news! Adolfo wants to get an angel reading. He has an appointment with Steffany tomorrow."

"What? Whoa...are you serious? Okay, this is big. But I'll bet you he backs out. In fact, I'll drink a glass of your green gunk if he actually goes through with it. No! Make that two glasses!"

"Okay, you're on. I think he will do it, but if he backs out, I'll...eat a bag of donuts!" I said. "Vegan of course..."

Julie rolled her eyes. "Vegan donuts are health food. You have to at least wash them down with Diet Coke!"

After Julie left, all that talk about margaritas, French fries, and donuts gave me a craving for something decadent to munch on, but my stomach was acting up again, bloated with sharp pains. Oddly, I thought of the time Sonia told me that I was energetically shifting to the new earth. A hardness in my solar plexis felt the same now as it did then. I settled for a cup of tea, and as I took a kettle out of the cupboard, a familiar pain shot through my right arm. Too much work on the computer? Arthritis? I just didn't feel right.

The night had grown chilly, so I took my cup of tea into the bedroom, snuggled under a blanket, and sipped. Toasty warm, I lay down with a small magnet on my forehead that I'd purchased on Etsy. It was supposed to help alkalize the system and open the third eye. I'd been wearing it every day for a few hours but hadn't had a breakthrough. Yet. Thoughts of Julie stayed with me. The City of Angels was a tough place to date, as I'd witnessed up close for over a decade. So what was wrong with Julie taking a slice of happiness where she could find it, even if it happened to be at Dunkin Donuts with a married fireman?

I've realized that each one of us treks along on his or her own path, sometimes gliding smoothly, sometimes stumbling over the rocks and falling, but as one study confirmed, most of us wouldn't trade our lives with someone else's. We're okay being who we are. So, as long as we allow others to navigate their own path, and we stick to ours, I believe everything will work out for our highest good. Of course, that's a big *if*.

Adolfo got home from his private gig, entered the bedroom, saw me, and started to chuckle. "Marlita, you'd better take that thing off your forehead before you go insane."

My beloved was referring to the magnet on my head. His skepticism was back, and it looked like Julie would be spared the green gunk, and I'd be loading up on calories and artificial sweeteners tomorrow afternoon.

I worked on matchmaking all the next day, worried he would cancel, but, on schedule, he opened Skype for his angel reading with Steffany.

While Adolfo was having his reading, I went into my sanctuary, sat on my meditation cushion and lit a "magickal" candle in a last ditch effort to get the rights back to my creative project. My attorney had not let up in her demands that my rights had to revert to me, but the person in question did not want to let go unless I paid an exorbitant amount.

I acquired the candle from Panpipes Magical Marketplace, the oldest full service occult shop and "magickal" apothecary in Hollywood. The delightful owner of the shop, Vicky, is a classically trained occultist in many of the magical arts. She hand blends her alchemy incenses with the freshest herbs and organic essential oils. I had heard good things about Vicky and her Candle Magick skills, and I was hoping that eleven dollars and clear, focused intention would help things along. Vicky explained that it wasn't the candle that produced results, but my intention.

"Meditate with the candle and send positive, loving thoughts towards this person. Affirm that they are gently releasing their grip on your work, and returning it to you peacefully."

Forty-five minutes later, Adolfo was smiling thoughtfully as he came out of his studio.

"So, how did it go?"

"What a nice lady. The way Steffany speaks is so soothing, and she has a beautiful smile."

"Yes, she's wonderful, but what did you think of the session?"

"Well, she brought up things about my family, about when I was young, and some other stuff which rang true, but I still can't say I believe. I mean, I want to believe in angels, but I'll admit, I'm still not convinced. I guess I'm not ready to believe in this stuff yet. I need concrete evidence, and I just haven't seen it yet."

My face must have registered disappointment.

"It was a great experience, though," he added. "I'm glad I did it. Thank you for arranging it, mi amor. Steffany is a real sweetheart!"

I admit I was hoping that Adolfo would emerge as a converted angel believer, but just the fact that he asked for a reading and actually went through with it, AND enjoyed it, was a huge step. I was convinced that Steffany *was* the real deal, because her readings for me, as well as for Katt and a couple of her friends were spot on, as well as a beautiful reading she gave my me and mom together over Skype. Sitting on my mom's sofa on a rainy Seattle night, we listened with astonishment as Steffany transmitted messages from my brother, regarding my mom just getting her bathroom professionally painted, our recent hair appointments, my mom's decorative frog collection, and the atrium inside her house. But then again, we believed already and were open. Maybe our openness allows the intuitive to access our energy field and guides more easily.

Later that night, Adolfo surprised me by agreeing to try the board. I was ecstatic. "Now honey, I am thrilled that you are willing to try this, but you MUST put your skepticism aside, because if you don't believe it'll work, it won't."

"I'll be open; I'll believe," he assured me.

Right. Now *I* was the one with doubts.

We sat across from each other in my sanctuary, he on the love seat and me in my purple velvet chair, knee to knee with my Swami board in between us. I chose the Swami board because it was the largest and sturdiest, made of wood. I said my prayer of protection, called in my guides and angels and opened up the board for communication. Adolfo and I waited silently for something to happen. The planchette moved ever so slightly, and then stopped. I gave it about five minutes before I decided to try another board. I got out my Psychic Circle board, a colorful board made of cardboard designed by Amy Zerner. Nothing. I set the Psychic Circle aside and replaced it with one of Amy's other boards, the Enchanted Spell Board. The planchette moved around the board, but didn't spell anything that made any sense.

"Your moving it," said Adolfo.

"I SWEAR TO GOD I AM NOT MOVING IT!" I was so desperate for something real and tangible to happen with Adolfo to finally prove that this stuff is real, that my own tense energy may have been the problem. I knew that I had a limited time, and if nothing happened here, he probably wouldn't give it another shot.

"Ugghh. Okay, hang on," I said as I switched out the board yet again, this time with my large wooden board with a beautiful angel in the middle. "This one is super powerful."

Adolfo sat patiently. Twenty minutes had passed. I had to hand it to him; at least he was giving this a valiant chance.

The planchette moved in circles around the board and then stopped. "You're moving it," Adolfo said again.

"No, I'm not, I swear. You have to believe me."

"Okay, honey, I think that's enough. I tried."

"No... No... please, just wait. I traded out the angel board with my Emily The Strange board. This was my main everyday go-to board to talk with Murth on. I usually don't let other people touch it, but I needed to pull out the big guns."

Nothing.

Adolfo could see the disappointment in my expression.

"Okay, I'm sorry. I was patient. I gave it a half an hour," he said getting up.

"It's because you don't believe! That's why it won't work. You have to believe!"

Adolfo gave me a kiss on the top of the head, "Well, I tried to believe."

I silently thanked God, Jesus, and all the saints and angels for my Adolfo. Despite our ups and downs, we mostly had ups, and we had made a good life together. We both counted our blessings. It would turn out that he was more correct about the talking board than I wanted to believe, but I didn't know that then. I was aware of a nagging stomach pain that would also turn out to be a possible indicator of what was actually going on.

Before I drifted off to sleep, I thought of an affirmation in Florence Scovil Shinn's, *The Game of Life and How To Play It*.

Marla Martenson

I give thanks for this perfect day, miracle shall follow miracle and wonders shall never cease.

Some Uninvited Guests

"There has to be evil so that good can prove its purity above it."
~ The Buddha

We Californians welcomed the late fall days of cold rainy weather, and along with the blessing of badly needed rain came news. My attorney emailed me concerning the rights to my creative project. She'd done a great job, remaining steadfastly fair and logical, never relenting, and never giving in to intimidation throughout the long, drawn-out process. I was almost afraid to open the email, but I took a deep breath and read it.

All rights would revert to me—and for an amount considerably less than what was asked. Amazing! Hallelujah! Something had managed to shake loose the pernicious grip on my work, and I couldn't ignore the timing of the victory, which coincided with Vicky's Candle Magick. The candle process had allowed me to focus my intentions of love, fairness, and resolution even if it meant letting go—a powerful dynamic I would never again ignore.

I'd begun to wonder, though, when the candle that Hovik the warlock dressed for Julie hadn't helped her much at all. It dawned on me why. Intent is the key. One can't just expect the candle to do all of the work. Julie hoped her candle would work like a birthday candle, making a wish and blowing out the flame. The wish would come true with no effort on the part of the birthday girl. But Julie's desire conflicted with her logical intent. She wanted to magically stop thinking about Sergio, but in her heart, she was still in love with him. Her true wish was that he would return her affection—whereupon she would dash across the street into his waiting arms.

If I had a current wish, it would be to experience a spiritual breakthrough. I'd been so focused on communicating with spirits that I felt with every intention and open chakra, I was on the verge. I would soon be channeling, maybe that very weekend.

I donned a raincoat and drove up to Topanga Canyon to a place called The 1909. Its intimate amphitheater nestled beneath tall live-oaks. The trees and a vast lawn, dubbed "the meadow," smelled woodsy and fresh in the rain, perfect weather for an indoor weekend workshop. The outdoor serenity, visible through large windows, filled the airy spaces inside.

I'd be spending two days with the Yale-educated channeler, Paul Selig with about forty other spiritual seekers, all of us eager to learn something new about the Universe from Paul's non-physical "guides" after responding to his website saying that over the two-day experience, we would:

- Receive individual instruction and teaching from Paul's Guides
- Become attuned to a higher frequency in a way that you can trust and feel
- Learn to send and receive healing energies
- Develop your own abilities as an empath
- Free yourself from patterns of limitation and fear
- Gain tools to transform your life and awaken to your own divine nature

My goals exactly, especially the attunements to higher frequencies. I figured that if I could raise my vibration, I would be able to bypass the spirit boards and establish direct contact with my guides, maybe even channel them. After a few exercises that morning, Paul delivered lectures via his guides that proved much more spellbinding in person than those seen on the Internet. He echoes what he hears in a whisper and then repeats it audibly. He says, "It's not very graceful to watch." Then the second day brought an entirely different experience, and not in the way I'd expected.

Paul opened to questions from the group, and we asked him or the guides more specifics about the teachings. He is not only a channel, but also "a medium for the living." I'd never seen this before, but Paul has the unique ability to step-into and "become" the people his clients ask about, often taking on their personalities and physical characteristics as he "hears" them telepathically. I asked a question about one of the teachings that the guides had given us, about non-judgment. Fighting back tears, I admitted that I felt like my whole life was entrenched in judgment because as a matchmaker, my male clients were so persnickety that I had to judge and rate the women like a choice cut of beef. How could I lead a spiritual life judging others' appearances all day?

"Come on up," said Paul.

I jumped out of my chair and stood about seven feet in front of Paul, the others seated in a wide circular row around the room. Paul explained that he was going to tune into me energetically. He started talking, taking on my characteristics and mannerisms and was speaking as if he were me.

"First of all, I'm hearing, 'I hate everyone! I hate everyone! These guys sign up for six months or a year and then their membership is up and no one is happy in the end. They think they know what they want, but they don't...It's a joke!'"

OMG! Paul had tuned right into me, and he was spot on.

"Yes..." I felt my cheeks reddening. "That's exactly what I say to myself when a client is being particularly challenging and none of the women are "hot enough" for his taste. Sometimes I just want to throw all of my client's files in the trash and light them on fire! And yes, the guys sign up for six months to a year, and many are unhappy in the end. The exact words in my head are often, 'It's a joke!'"

Paul approached me. "I'm called to come to your throat. Is it okay if I touch your throat?"

"Absolutely!" I was ecstatic to be having one-on-one time with Paul. I'd already been pummeled with bamboo sticks, cup-suctioned, and treated with leeches. Whatever he had in mind would be just fine with me.

Paul said that there was something in my throat and he started to pull out energy. He backed up about six feet and put his hands out. I literally felt a whoosh of cold air come off of me from about waist high.

Then he asked another attendee to stand next to him and hold out his hand so he could feel the air too.

"This is old stuff; let it go, release..." said Paul. "I am hearing fourteen years."

"I've been a matchmaker for fourteen years," I said, tears running down my cheeks.

"Let it go... here it comes, here it comes." The cold air kept flowing.

I let it all go and felt lighter and lighter. Back in my chair, I felt utterly amazed.

The woman seated to my left leaned toward me. "I saw energy coming off you. It looked like dark smoke!"

At lunchtime, a woman who had been sitting about fifteen feet behind me said, "I felt the temperature turn cold in the room when Paul was pulling the energy off you. And you looked different afterwards, lighter."

The weekend was definitely life-changing, and although I felt conflicted in my feelings about matchmaking, I focused on my profound gratitude to my clients that provided me the money to be able to take amazing transformational workshops such as Paul's. I didn't exactly feel the higher frequencies yet that I was hoping for, but I believed that with continued meditation and studying the books Paul channeled, things would shift and change in a more powerful way.

Ever since the night Adolfo mistook my heavy breathing for me pleasuring myself when the energy shot through my crown chakra, I had continued to feel a considerable stimulation at the top of my head, as if someone were touching my hair. My stomach still caused me pain and bloating, along with the sore right arm. It all felt connected somehow.

Fortunately, Tauheedah had generously offered everyone on the healing team a complimentary crystal healing/clearing to kick off the New Year and celebrate the expansion of the center. I had to force myself to keep the appointment since my stomach was really bothering me.

I entered the healing room and sat across from Tauheedah on a folding chair. She asked me how I was feeling, and I explained the odd symptoms.

"I wonder if I have parasites. I juice a lot and eat lots of fresh fruits and vegetables. Oh, and I kiss my dog a lot."

Tauheedah smiled, I knew that she was a dog-lover, so I figured she would understand. "Ok, let me tune into your energy field," she said. "I'll be able to find out what's going on with that."

We both closed our eyes and took some deep breaths. Tauheedah connected with the non-physical.

"I'm hearing something about you using some kind of a board."

"Yes." Wow. Was her connection with my guides, hers, or angels or what? "I connect with my angels on a talking board."

"Do you cleanse the board?"

"No, I only cleansed it once. I did a whole ritual with sage, and prayers, etc."

"You need to cleanse it. Have you been seeing psychics?" she asked.

I explained that yes, I had, and had attending many workshops, practicing and learning new modalities. I also told her about my YouTube channel gaining popularity and that I was interviewing lots of psychics, channelers, and healers, many of whom had offered sessions and readings.

"They're saying that the problem is with the board, and also someone you have been working with, maybe a psychic, I don't know." I told her about the one person I had been working with the most, Jimmy Mack.

"Jimmy feels good to me. If you feel good with him, keep working with him. And are you using some kind of psychic tool?"

"Well, I have been wearing a magnet on my forehead for the past couple of weeks to try to open my third eye." Dang, I thought, nothing gets by Tauheedah. This woman is tuned in.

She looked off to the side, listening. "Stop using it for now."

"Okay."

Tauheedah gave me a meaningful look. "You have an infiltration."

I nodded. "That's what I thought. Parasites, huh?"

"No, you have an infiltration of low-vibrational entities. There are six of them."

My mouth hung open. Holy guacamole. I was possessed?

Tauheedah led me to the table, and I lay down on my back. She placed a mask over my eyes, and went to work placing crystals on and around my body. By their weight, I could feel that she was using the really big crystals. No little piddly-ass stones. Apparently, I needed the big guns. She vigorously shook her rattle, breaking up energy and clearing over and over again with her hands and her breath.

"There are two more," she said, continuing to clear.

Shit! "There are eight?"

"Yes. And Marla, your guides have been disabled. They have been kept away."

I told Tauheedah about the night that the powerful energy came in through my crown chakra. It suddenly made sense.

"Yes, that was the main entity. They come in through the crown. There are two more, one in your throat."

I shared about how Paul also said that something was in my throat, and told her about the cold air and dark energy coming off me.

Tauheedah explained that the entities had energetic "wiring" wrapped around my jaw and behind my ears. She worked diligently with a crystal wand to remove the entity in my throat. It seemed especially stubborn.

"My right arm has been hurting."

"I'm not surprised. There is an entity between your heart chakra and your rib cage."

She removed the last entity and continued to clear me. I felt a cool menthol sensation at my crown chakra.

"Marla, I've been working an hour. I need another fifteen minutes." For someone doing free sessions, she was being amazingly thorough. "Are you okay?"

I urged her to continue. There was no way I was getting off that table until the entities were completely cleared.

Tauheedah continued shaking her rattle and clearing with her breath and hands, "Okay...okay...yes...your guides are back. Here they come."

"I have a headache."

This was all too incredible. I tried to wrap my mind around this.

I started to shiver. I was freezing. Tauheedah helped me to sit up, and she did some clearing on my back.

"Marla, you need another session. Come back in two weeks and we'll build your energy field back up, and fill it with love and light. Don't do any psychic work for now, not even meditation. Take a salt bath tonight and eat very light. I'm glad you came in."

How on earth could this have happened to me? I wondered what Tauheedah thought of me. Maybe she wouldn't want me on the healing team anymore. I had been so diligent in my studies and efforts to raise my vibration. I guess I had been naïve, thinking that everything was all unicorns and rainbows. I felt I was above the dark energies, untouchable in a way. Apparently not. What if I hadn't come in for a clearing?

Tauheedah said that these entities first came two years ago. Would they have completely taken me over, or pushed me to do something out of line with my integrity, or disintegrate my health? I shuddered at the thought. I was in awe of Tauheedah's powers to remove dark entities, and I pondered whether I would ever achieve her status as a healer. I was good at getting stagnant energy flowing, opening up the chakras, and infusing life force energy, but detecting a dark entity and actually removing it? Hell...I didn't have a clue.

I left the center in a daze, but my stomach was no longer bloated, and the pain had left my arm. I walked across the street to Whole Foods and purchased some lavender bath salt and some Indian food from the food bar.

I wasted no time when I got home. I prayed to Archangel Michael for protection—prayer being an acceptable part of Tauheedah's healing regimen. I grabbed my board and saged the heck out of it. Macie followed me from room to room as I beat my pink tribal drum all over the house to break up any existing low energy, followed by burning sage in every room, making sure to waft it with a green turkey feather into every corner. Of course I burned the sage for an extra few minutes in my sanctuary, since that was where I did all of my spiritual work.

Next, I filled the tub with hot water and lavender salt and had a nice soak. Macie wasn't used to seeing me take a bath. She stood on her hind legs peering into the tub to make sure I was okay.

I crawled into bed and stared at the ceiling. The past two years played out in my mind like a movie. This whole journey that I began with Julie, I wouldn't have traded it for the world. I'd learned more about myself in those two years than I'd ever imagined. My strengths, my weaknesses, my passion, desires, capabilities and creativity had all surfaced anew like a discovery at an archeology site.

I thought about my board. Over the past couple of years, many people had told me to be careful, or suggested not using it at all, for fear of lower energies or demons coming through. I'd laughed it off since I'd had only wonderful experiences with the board, although now the sessions that seemed odd, even then, I'd thought might be "trickster" spirits. I now wondered about those sessions.

Karen Dahlman and I had made lots of videos, discussing the insightful communication one could experience by using the board as a serious spiritual tool. Of course we were careful to tell people to open and close the board with a prayer, and to treat it as a sacred tool. If an individual felt trepidation, was in turmoil, or sensed darkness, he or she shouldn't use it.

I also thought about some close girlfriends who had gone through some very difficult times recently. One friend had lost her dear mother, and one was in financial straits with a possibility of ending up homeless. I spent many a candlelight evening with my board, giving them readings over the phone, connecting with Murth and their angels, imparting insightful messages and advice. They took notes, listening in awe at the wisdom and love that flowed through the angels, giving them hope and some understanding. There was no doubt in their minds that the sessions were not only loving, but positive and profound. I knew this experience was real and valuable.

If Tauheedah was right, the low vibrational energies were with me at the time I gave the readings. This must mean that my energy and connection to angels and spirit were stronger than the low vibrational energy's hold on me. But still, I wondered if I should continue making videos with Karen about Ouija Boards. I was so confused. I emailed Karen and Grace and explained what happened.

Karen offered the following advice about spirit entities:

> I do suggest that you set rules up around your room and sleep. State out loud that they cannot come in your room and can only come when you are aware and with the assistance of your guides. Years ago I did this and have never had a problem since.
>
> Also, I believe that you can be empathic and take in other energies, but that is just something to learn (how to separate from that) in order to not let that infiltrate your system. Learn and know that you can be around all kinds of negativity and NOT have it infiltrate your system. It's something to learn. I used to work in the prison system as a contract therapist. I learned quickly to NOT allow their negativity/energies/attachments to affect me. It was a technique I learned within

my training. You can go into the darkest of places and NEVER EVER be affected because you will KNOW your center.

Karen had used the board for over forty years and was still as passionate about it as ever. Linda Salvin, the skilled psychic and healer, had no qualms about using it, nor Linda Deir.

Grace also responded to my email:

> I mentioned this briefly in the workshop you came to last year, when I talked about the two dark years in my transformation process. I saw dark energies around me. It is real. I absolutely didn't believe that way, just like you. I thought everything was light and no dark. It does come down to knowing and then FOCUS, focus on the intention of the highest light always. Protection is KEY.

I didn't want to give up using the board. I enjoyed it too much. I just needed to protect myself better. Even though Tauheedah recommended that I stay off the board for a couple of weeks, I just couldn't help myself. I needed to know what Murth thought of all this. I would be quick. I went into my sanctuary and pulled out my angel board.

I commenced with my own version of an opening ritual that Karen taught me. I imagined a protective white light surrounding me. I stated only that which comes from the place of illumination, truth, clarity, and wisdom was allowed to come through the portal of communication.

White light surrounds me, including Macie, and the whole house and property. I give thanks to you Murth in advance for your wisdom. The white light is with us. We may now begin.

Murth came through immediately.

"Murth, what happened, how did I get an infiltration?"

> *Yes, Marla, you were a target because you didn't ask for protection every time. And also you went on another board in that shop in Canoga Park and boy it did let a bad energy in. You were only on it for a short time but it came in quickly. Be careful and always ask for protection. Your guides were disabled and could not get them to leave. There were ten like Tauheedah said.*

"The energy that came in that night, was that one of the low energies?"

> *Yes, that was the main one. Very scary stuff my dear! Angels love you so much. We are here for you. They [the low-energy entities] are gone now but they would love to come back. Be vigilant in your cleansing rituals and stay away from random boards.*

"Is this board safe?"

> *Yes, this board is safe as it is your special board to communicate with us angels on. And I want to say that you are a magnificent human being, just a bit too trusting sometimes. Even the spirit world can have some bad seeds, so just be*

aware. You are a very sweet and trusting soul Marla. Question everything. I love you.

On my way back to bed, I remembered Deborah King's book, ENTANGLED in Darkness, SEEKING the Light. I grabbed it off the shelf, hoping to get some more insight on dark energies. In chapter one, she discusses the forces of dark energy. She explained the different types which are psychic attack, energy vampires, slime, cords, a vector of force, and possession.

It sounded like I was the target of a vector of force, which is a stream of energy, which can enter a hole in your energy field without your consent. Vectors are always dark and are very difficult for a recipient to disconnect from without professional help. Tauheedah had described "wires," so maybe some cords were also involved. Deborah King also explained that all day every day we are making choices and on our plane of free will, everything counts. Each decision either raises you up energetically or lowers your vibration.

The week that followed, I connected with my tribe of other healers, and spiritual seekers and discovered that most of them had very similar experiences at one point or another on their journey. I interviewed a lovely woman named Marie-Ange Faugérolas for my YouTube show. She wrote a book titled Angels: the Definitive Guide To Angels From Around The World. She first saw an angel at the age of four as well as some ghosts in her grandmother's house in France. She, like Steffany, knows as much as can be known on the subject of angels.

After the interview I asked Marie-Ange what she knew about dark energies and told her about my recent experience removing my uninvited guests.

"I actually felt ashamed that I somehow brought this on myself," I told her.

"Oh, my goodness, no, you have nothing to be ashamed about. Evil exists and the angels are fighting every minute for us against evil on this planet. The angels are very busy!" She explained that she also had many encounters with dark energy that attempted to attach themselves to her as well. I asked her about the many workshops I had attended. I thought that maybe I could have picked up something there.

She agreed that when a person attends workshops and events with many people, there are lots of spirits hanging around, and one can become attached that way.

"But the most common way they get in, is when you are down, depressed, or going through a hard time in your life, or using alcohol or drugs, because that causes holes in your aura, which makes you a target for low-vibrational entities to enter."

I felt so much better after our conversation. My feelings quickly shifted from shame to that of a certified cardholder in a private club—a spiritual adept, who went to the dark side and made it through. Yet I had to know more about these low-vibrational energies/dark spirits. Were they just the un-evolved souls of rotten people who had died and couldn't make it into the Light? Demon agents of Satan? Aliens? Beings from weird dimensions? All of the above? Figments on which to blame our shortcomings and mistakes? I had to know more.

Battle of the Psychics

"Life is not divided into good and bad, positive and negative, nice and naughty. Life is an olio, a mixture, a cauldron swirling with the tides of our changing desires." ~ Susun Weed

Nightmares had been showing in my dreamland theater for two nights in a row, starring the low-vibrational entities. In the first one, the head honcho told me in a menacing tone that he (it felt like a male energy) would never leave me. In the second dream, I was using a Ouija board, and I asked the entity, "who are you?" And just as the planchette moved to spell his name, I woke myself up because I didn't want to know.

The next night was Saturday. I was exhausted, so I went to bed around eight. Lying on my side, I was just starting to drift off to sleep when I felt that mo-fo's energy enter me again. I was immediately paralyzed and heard garbled voices in my left ear.

Through my "third eye" I saw quick flashes of images and then a visage that looked especially menacing, a man with an oddly lizard-shaped face, old and angry.

I couldn't move or open my mouth, so I mentally pleaded for Jesus and Archangel Michael to help me. About fifteen seconds later, the entity left my body, and I could move. I rolled over onto my back and turned on the TV to take my mind off of what happened. I immediately felt energy moving across my thighs, a tingly sensation.

I had enough. "GET OUT OF HERE!" I got up out of bed, went into my sanctuary and got some sage. I burned it all over the house and saged my body. Then I grabbed my rosary with a large crucifix on the end, my selenite wand, and slipped on my wooden bracelet from Mexico that has a large image of Jesus on it. I went back to bed and placed the crucifix and the crystal on my chest.

Adolfo came home from work around 1:00 AM. "What's that smell?"

"Sorry honey, I know you hate the smell of sage, but the entities came back."

His face hardened. "The entities came back. Right. What kind of bullshit is this? Marlita, this has got to stop! I tried to be open-minded about all of this stuff, but this has gone too far."

"Adolfo, I'm sorry, but it's true, I was scared shitless. They're bothering me! They were touching my legs!"

"Touching your legs? Come on!"

"I know it sounds nuts, but please believe me. Ugghh, Never mind. Just go to sleep. I have it handled."

Of course, I certainly didn't blame Adolfo for thinking I was losing it.

The next morning, I was making coffee when Adolfo came into the kitchen.

"Are the entities here for breakfast?" he said with a grin. "Maybe they want some tofu."

I refused to laugh and polished off my green gunk to make sure he couldn't see any kind of smile lurking.

"Aye Marlita..." At least his anger from last night was gone. "You are something else. Entities. Anyway, I told you a demon was going to come through that board, but you wouldn't believe me."

"Honey, okay, I'll admit, you were *sort* of right." I hurried on before he could gloat. "It certainly wasn't a demon, though. These are low-level energies—tricksters—looking to attach to a vulnerable host. I'm guessing it happens all the time. If many people had low vibrational attachments, it sure would explain road rage on the 405."

"You just don't want to hear *I told you so.*"

"Well...I do admit I should have been more diligent in cleansing my energy field and using protection every time I got on the board. It's a learning process."

Shaking his head, he poured himself a cup of coffee. "Well, I hope you feel okay today." With that, he retreated to his studio.

I went into my office and shot off an email to Tauheedah explaining what happened and what actions I took to get them to leave. Her reply:

> Hi, Marla. Thanks for update. You responded powerfully. They're trying to bully you to draw you into fear. Stay strong! They don't and can't own your energy. We will purge this!
> Blessings!
> Tauheedah

The time away from my talking boards, meditations at my altar, and other spiritual work felt oddly mundane. I'd only risked the one conversation with Murth, but I missed my regular conversations with her, and I wanted to keep as much high-vibrational energy around me as I could muster. I'd learned how wonderful and empowering that feels, and I never want to be without it. So, I asked Vicky from Pan-pipes to dress a candle for me to attract new and exciting opportunities, hoping that wouldn't count as spiritual work that might open channels for connection with the wrong non-physical beings.

Finally, the follow-up session with Tauheedah came, and I was excited. I felt that the entities had gone, but her assessment and affirmation of that was important to me.

Tauheedah used her rattle vigorously, breaking up energy and clearing. She was rebuilding my energy field.

"Oh Marla, your energy is *so* much lighter!"

I was curious how the entities found me again after she removed them and sent them into the ground in the first session.

"The guides are saying that there were fragments still stationed in your bedroom and they wanted to reattach. And they are saying when you called for Jesus to come and help, he did come and chased those entities out."

Just as I'd felt cold and depleted when Tauheedah had drawn the entities out, I now felt warm and definitely light. It felt so good to know that I'm never alone. I can call on Jesus or the angels and they will come to help.

"I might have glimpsed the main entity," I said. "It flashed in my mind's eye. It almost looked reptilian."

Tauheedah explained that in the New Age community, there is much talk of Reptilians, a very dangerous alien species bent on the domination of Earth. Ah, I thought but didn't say, the Gorn. Those old Star Trek episodes were onto something. I was going to need Captain Kirk, in that case.

Give me angels any day, and I'll believe them, along with the world's major cultures. There are Zoroastrian angels; Buddhists call on their *devas* such as Kwan Yin; in Thailand they're called *nangfah*. Hindus look to angels referred to as the "shining ones." The Jewish faith identifies the Malachim and other angels. Angels are one of the six pillars of Islam. I'll even believe in fairies, since many cultures describe tiny magical beings: European fairies, Asian sprites, Incan, Hawaiian, and more. But alien power-hungry spirit-reptiles? Not so much. As to the image I saw, I think I'd consider the possibility that my subconscious was trying to come up with an image that matched the way the entities made me feel. That's the kind of explanation Seth (channeled by Jane Roberts) would no doubt offer.

"So, Tauheedah," I asked, "is it common that healers and seekers often acquire low vibrational attachments?"

She agreed it was. "Actually, I think going through this was necessary to take you to the next level as a healer. Now you know what it feels like and can be more sympathetic to others who are going through this. But as you see, we are all responsible for protecting our own energy; it's very important."

I realized right then and there that I needed to step things up for my own protection. I needed to work at my altar daily through prayer and meditation, not just fit in here and there between matchmaking. I knew for a fact that Tauheedah was on top of her spiritual practice daily, and it showed. She set the highest standards in this area.

I couldn't begin my new regimen yet however. Tauheedah said that I should take a few weeks off from giving healings in order to let the new energy settle in my body and integrate. I decided to take this time to go deeper into study about energy and how to protect myself in a more efficient way, although I had no idea just how deep I would delve or how vastly the opinions among some of the extra sensory perception specialists would differ.

I began with a woman who was named among the World's Greatest Psychics and profiled in twelve books, Elizabeth Joyce. Spiritual/energy healer, astrologer, counselor, medium, clairvoyant, author, and more, she has assisted the FBI and police in many missing person's cases. (She also predicted Gore would become President and Clinton would resign, and her percentage of accuracy has apparently never been tested.) Her book *The New Spiritual Chakras and How to Work with Them* is still one of my go-to books to learn about the Chakra system. She is definitely knowledgeable and experienced in mystical matters, and I was excited to read her books. I interviewed her, but when I asked her opinion on the Ouija Board, she exclaimed, "Ouija Boards should be burned and never used. When you use a Ouija Board you can be hosted. Angels don't come through an angel board; they never have, and they never will."

I showed her my little board and explained that I have only had good experiences with it. She was beside herself. "Why is it red and black? Oh my goodness, my heart is beating so fast. You will NEVER have a good experience with that board!"

She went on, "Every single time you have an experience with that board, you are putting a black spot on your soul! Because whatever good you think that is coming to you, is not coming to you. You are getting messages from something ugly and dark! Get rid of that board immediately!"

When I questioned why I had only gotten wonderful, loving, positive messages for the past *two years*, she replied, "to gain your trust so they could eventually take you completely over without protest."

"But even Jane Roberts met Seth through the Ouija Board," I said.

Elizabeth wasn't having any of it. "No she didn't! No she didn't!"

I was shaken to the core by her reaction and response. She was a lovely lady and had reasons for her opinion. I also knew that she was just looking out for my best interest, and her feelings about the board were shared by many, but giving up the new modality I'd worked so patiently to cultivate? Give up Murth? I felt in my heart that Murth was real, and not a trickster. I couldn't yet bring myself to abandon this precious connection with the spirit world. It would be too great a loss. Yet Elizabeth was highly experienced. Could I just ignore her? No. I needed to think about this and dig deeper in my research.

It didn't seem at all logical that Murth would spend two years telling me loving messages and perceptive insights only to twist them into something evil. There were nights I was tired after a long day and wanted to communicate with Murth, but she routinely turned me away. "Not now Marla, you are tired. Go to bed, we can talk tomorrow. I love you. Xoxo." Now, I would think a "demon" would want me to be tired and worn down so that it could take advantage of me, not tell me to get some rest.

I was also pretty sure that Jane Roberts had used the Ouija Board, but just for due diligence, I scoured the Internet, read articles, and ordered a copy of *Seth Speaks* on my Kindle. There was the confirmation on page two. Jane Roberts talks about meeting Seth on the Ouija Board. Her psychic initiation started in 1963 when she was writing poetry. Her consciousness left her body, and when she returned, she discovered that her hands had produced an automatic script titled "The Physical Universe as Idea Construction." Soon after this episode, Roberts suddenly began recalling her dreams, including two that were highly precognitive, the first, as far as she knew, that she'd ever experienced.

Because of that experience, she began to research psychic activity. In late 1963, Jane and her husband Rob started experimenting with a Ouija board as part of the research for a book. According to the couple, on December 2, 1963 they began to receive coherent messages from a male personality who eventually identified himself as Seth, an "energy personality essence" no longer focused in physical form. Soon after, Jane reported that she was hearing the messages in her head. The first seven sessions were entirely with the Ouija board. The three-hour session on the evening of Jan. 2, 1964 was the first where she began to dictate the messages instead of using the Ouija board. For a while she still opened her sessions with the board, but finally was able to abandon it.

I felt that I needed another professional opinion on the subject. World famous psychic, Linda Salvin was my friend with whom I used the Ouija Board to communicate with Linda's guide, a famous deceased musician who prefers to remain anonymous.

Let's just call him *Mike*.

I sent Linda a message and told her I needed to see her ASAP since my very soul was apparently hanging in the balance of good and evil.

"Come on over," she said, to my great relief. "We can talk to Mike."

I jumped in my Toyota and raced to her home. I installed myself at her dining room table, and with a view of the bougainvillea around her fountain and her beautiful pool calming me, I recounted the whole story from the day I first felt the dark energy to my conversation with psychic Elizabeth Joyce.

"Linda," I concluded, "you obviously approve of the Ouija Board, but what is your take on dark energy and Ouija use? I don't want to give it up. Gosh, I mean, the fun I have with you and Karen, and also on my own, the great messages we get...it's been some of the most interesting times of my life. Of course, I want to stay safe, but if I *have* been misled by dark energy...well, I'm willing to be wrong. This is all so confusing."

Linda listened, and her little dog Penny watched us attentively from under the table. Linda's small parrots, Rainbow and Starlight, added a lively soundtrack.

"The Ouija Board is a valuable tool when properly used," she said. "We can connect with spirits from beyond. The wisdom and spiritual insight received is not human. I've had numerous board sessions over a twenty-year period where over 90% of the messages proved to be true over a period of time. My mother, grandmother, some friends, and one soul in particular whom I'd never met in life channel through the board and have communicated amazing and astonishing messages of truth and wisdom that I could not have possibly made up. As a professional psychic/medium I can attest to the beauty and accuracy of the Ouija Board."

"Can you share a couple of examples, Linda?"

"Just recently, I had a conflict with a family member I feared might take a few months to reconcile, but Mike said it would resolve during the next week. Four days later that's exactly what happened!"

She laughed as she revealed that Mike had long ago told her she'd be on a few radio shows, but she absolutely didn't believe him. Now, she's a radio host veteran of seventeen years. "Mike told a friend of mine which real estate company she would be working for, and he was right. He also predicted that a client would move from Fullerton to Simi Valley. He is incredibly accurate."

"Wow, that is amazing." I was feeling much better. "Remember when Mike told me that one of my clients was problematic and an egomaniac and that he would be asking for his money back? I forgot to tell you that actually happened. Unfortunately! So, it stands to reason that if there are rotten people in the world, there can be rotten spirits as well."

Linda explained about negative energy. "Personally, I'd been afraid of the Ouija board until I learned to properly use it. It's true that novices and people trying the board for fun or under the influence of drugs or alcohol bring in negative entities and can be harmed. We can draw in negative spirits if we're not protected and are disrespectful of the spiritual world and the board. The Ouija board is not a toy. We humans have souls, we have the ability to communicate with spirit, we can use the board as a tool but we need to protect ourselves and our lives when working with the unknown."

I asked her what should be done if that happens.

"Some of my clients have actually paid me to speak to some of these entities," she said. "I've spent hours with certain friends, Ouija-ing with as much passion as some people bring to playing bridge." She added that such a session often gave her a backache, depleted her potassium levels, and exhausted her.

"Have you ever experienced the dark energies?" I asked.

She admitted she had. "But I've learned how to identify certain spirits. The energy is dark and cold. Words and messages are negative and frightening, and a sense of evil hovers in the room. By simply asking them to leave and waving my hand over the board in a way that cleanses and resets the spiritual connection, I have been successful in keeping the darkness out. The loving and safe spirits can be especially comforting when the board is used properly. I love the Ouija board and am very selective about which spirits I allow to communicate."

Next, Linda lit some candles, took out her board, and Mike, her special channeled entity, came in. I asked him his take on everything.

Hi, Marla. Don't listen to Elizabeth. I am real, not negative. The dark energies that were attached to you came from the board and people and also from not knowing how to protect yourself. Get saged.

I asked about my little black and red board. "Should I burn it or get rid of it, or can I cleanse it? I do like it."

Your red and black board has bad energy for your spirit. You can cleanse it, but it's better not to use it.

Interesting... Mike agreed with Elizabeth Joyce on that point. "Which board should I use?"

The blue one with the angel on it is better.

I hadn't mentioned this board to Linda. So, you see? Real deal! Otherwise, how would Mike know about my blue angel board? I had only brought over my little red and black one once when Karen and I went over to Linda's the year prior for an "Ouija day."

"And you have told me before that Murth is real, and she is my angel, but I am asking again. Is Murth the real deal?"

Murth dictates truth.

I felt so much better and confident in Murth. I thanked Linda and left, but even though I felt good about everything after hearing both sides from bonafide professionals, I kept digging and found this on the Internet.

> *You probably won't hear too much about this in AA meetings, but Bill Wilson, the co-founder of Alcoholics Anonymous, often used a Ouija board to contact spirits. For a while, his participation in AA was deeply affected by his involvement with the "witchboard." Wilson claimed that he received the twelve-step method directly from a spirit without the board and wrote it down. Bill was consistently a spiritualist, going through life with AA's Big Book in one hand and an Ouija board in the other. In the basement, Bill W. had a "Spook Room" where he would communicate with the dead. (Source: My Name Is Bill: Bill Wilson–His Life and the Creation of Alcoholics Anonymous, by Susan Cheever)*

On my path to enLITEnment, I have come to the realization that I can ask "experts," and I can delve, research, and dig, but in the end, I must be the one to choose what to believe and act accordingly because our main connection to Source lies within each of us. Nothing would exist without this connection. One metaphysical friend says that without the presence of Source energy, subatomic particles wouldn't exist, let alone zip around a nucleus of dense energy, allowing substance and matter, the cosmos, and all within it to exist. Living beings would certainly not exist without animation from the energy of Source—our basic spirits, tiny fragments of Infinite Source.

Polarity, yin and yang, drives change and growth. It is essential. So, everyone sees things differently and has their own opinions based on childhood, background, religion, experience, and conditioning. We are each a walking construct of these things. They are essential, and yet they can also lock us into narrow beliefs that cause us to judge others from the context of our own framework. Frameworks can also harden into prisons.

I recall being amused by the conflicting opinions of my grandmothers when I was a little girl. As a kid, every August my parents bought my brother and me some new school clothes, which I excitedly showed off to both of my grandmothers at Sunday dinner. I took them each individually into my room. My Grandma Martenson stood in front of the open closet, hand on cheek, shaking her head and tsk-tsking. "You have absolutely nothing. We need to buy you more clothes." My Grandma Reed had a different reaction. Ever so frugal, she shook her head in disapproval, with a pained look on her face, "Oh my goodness, *so* many clothes."

So, when psychics heatedly disagree on the nature of the spirit world, they may be looking at the same closet, yet seeing two entirely different things.

The extent to which an individual can feel connected to Source is the extent to which an individual recognizes that everything is a fascinating and miraculous materialization of Source and is therefore connected to Self. *Self* is a tiny part of it all. Self is a tiny avatar of Source, which is why the spiritual journey is a journey within. And so I must meditate to connect with my inner Source. I must do what feels right to me, what brings me joy, inspiration, and sparks my creativity. As long as I am enveloped in light and feel LITE, I am on the right path.

Simply a Different Path

"Today I see beauty everywhere I go, in every face I see, in every single soul." ~ *Kevyn Aucoin*

After all the drama around the spiritual infiltration by low vibrational beings, two events excited me. One of my clients booked a healing session and an angel reading as a gift for two sisters. This felt wonderfully validating but also worrisome because I didn't think enough time had elapsed, and I wasn't ready to open my channel to the occult again, especially with others involved. I hoped to recharge my psychic batteries, however, at the annual Conscious Life Expo. I was thrilled to be spending the whole day with Julie on our yearly excursion at its site, the LAX Hilton. The exposition occupies four exhibit halls and offers over 200 speakers, workshops, lectures and special events. To spiritual junkies like us, it's equivalent to a food addict in a bakery.

I pulled up to the curb in front of Julie's house and stepped out of the car.

Julie waved from across the street. "Hey, Marla," She was standing in the driveway of her neighbor's house. "I want you to meet Sergio."

Ah, at last, I would get to shake hands with the man who had short-circuited Julie's chakras for the past two years. Sergio had a friendly face, warm smile, and a midsection that suggested a preference to beer over green juice. "Nice to meet you, Marla."

Julie explained that we were going to the Conscious Life Expo.

"What's that?"

"It's a huge expo with psychics, healers, angel communicators, vegan food vendors, *and more!*"

Sergio rolled his eyes. "Well, ladies, good luck with THAT!"

Julie laughed it off, giddy just being in his presence. I knew that she'd been hanging out with Sergio as she had before the unfortunate camping trip. Lately, however, whenever we went somewhere together, much of the time was spent engrossed in her phone, texting him back and forth as if they were fifteen again. Don't get me wrong. I was happy that she and Sergio finally made up and could remain friends. It was clear he had no interest in a relationship, but she had her buddy back to debate politics and watch movies with. I prayed that she wouldn't be disappointed.

"Okay, so is he out of your system for the afternoon? Have you said all you need to say for now...or will you be texting him all day?"

"No...it's all good." She smiled sheepishly.

An hour later, we valet-parked and walked into the hotel. Julie had purchased our tickets online, so we donned our wristbands and entered a spacious hall, filled with vendors and a stage where a gal was playing the guitar and singing. The smell of Indian food wafted in the air, and my stomach grumbled. Unfortunately, at least twenty spiritual pilgrims lined up for Indian food, so I opted for a slice of vegan apple pie and a cup of organic coffee from a vendor downstairs.

I texted George Noory to find out where he was, and he told us to come upstairs in the Marina room where he was hosting a panel of experts for a discussion of "The Future of Humanity." We entered the packed room, and I ran smack dab into Alan Steinfeld of the show, "New Realties." I was so excited I practically accosted him. He sort of recognized me and remembered that Paul Selig had told him that I had interviewed him and that he enjoyed being on my show.

"Oh my gosh," I gushed. "And I just have to tell you how much I love *your* show. When I can't sleep at night, I put in my headphones and listen to your interviews."

"Really? You like my stuff? That is so sweet. We should do a show together," he said, as he gave me his number. SCORE!

Gliding on a cloud the rest of the day, Julie and I hit as many booths as possible. I controlled my spending as best I could, only purchasing a few new healing tools including a gemstone water bottle that contained rose quartz, amethyst, and clear quartz crystals in a "gempod" at the bottom of the bottle. I thought it would be nice to offer my Reiki clients a glass of crystal infused water after their session. Julie bought some organic hair thickening tonic, but unfortunately, the woman who sold it to her had trouble running her credit card and kept swiping and swiping. Julie told her to stop, but she was determined to get the sale. The result was Julie's card was charged six times and the bank put a hold on her card for the rest of the day. Julie was furious.

"I told her to just forget it, but she wouldn't give up."

"I think the Universe is trying to tell you something, because this is the third time something has happened at an event. Once you forgot your money, and another time, your card was declined, and now this."

"Oh my gosh, Marla, that's right. I guess I'm getting the message to stop spending, huh? I mean, how many psychic readings does a girl need? But it doesn't make me any less pissed off at that woman. I'm thinking of putting a stop payment and just keeping the products. She put the kybosh on my purchasing anything else!"

"If you really want something, I'll lend you the money."

"I know, but you shouldn't have to. Marla, I really need a drink. Do you mind? Come over to the bar with me, just one margarita."

Oh, no. A detour along a slippery slope. "Julie, are you sure? Don't let this incident get you down; you have been doing so well with your anti-drinking meetings."

"Just one...I promise..."

Mm-hmmm. I followed her into the hotel bar and actually ordered a margarita for myself, which was also not wise since I had recently recovered from a two-day hangover. My girlfriend Megan was in town from Australia. Megan had spent two weeks at a posh spa in Laguna Beach, eating super clean, hiking and doing yoga. She lost ten pounds and was feeling amazing. She then checked into a hotel in Beverly Hills so she could see a few friends in LA, and we met at Mastro's for dinner, our annual girls' night out. Before I even got there, she was texting me about her new favorite obsession, a salted caramel martini.

"That's all I thought about at the spa," she'd told me, "you have to try one."

We each ordered a martini (which was really like two because Mastro's gives *very* generous portions) then we split a second. Megan was correct in her assessment. The salted caramel martini was fabulous, a divine excursion of the taste buds, a trip to Cloudville. We enjoyed catching up and laughing over the time we went out to lunch a few years back, and the bartender, a washed up soap star, kept refilling our wine glasses. My golden rule, which was never drink and shop, didn't apply that day. My chardonnay-saturated noggin decided that my budget could accommodate a $250.00 Gucci belt. That indulgence still haunts me. I would just have to see the Expo's many exciting products as a test of character. Could I drink and resist such great temptations?

I was still kicking myself over an impulsive expenditure two years prior at the Expo when I fell prey to an East Indian "psychic." I stupidly handed over my credit card to be charged 250.00 for the "deluxe reading." The sheister gave me about ten minutes of "psychic reading time" and the rest was spent sorting through a tray of rings with various semi-precious stones, tempting me to spend yet another hundred bucks. I was so upset with myself that I vowed to never pay for a reading at an event again. However, there were plenty of other temptations and goodies to purchase such as crystals, jewelry, angelic sound healing, organic body products and lotions, one of a kind handmade clothing and accessories, books, tarot decks, and the list went on and on. I hoped I had developed more restraint over the past couple of years.

After only three sips of my margarita, I started to feel woozy. I needed distraction. "Julie, I can't tell you how excited I am about meeting Alan Steinfeld. He wants to do a show with me. In the YouTube world, it's called a *collab*."

"My, aren't you just down with the lingo! Cheers to that!" We clinked glasses.

The bartender was flirting with Julie, and must have wanted to impress her by giving us an extra shot in our drinks. I managed to back off, so Julie finished mine, her mood improving with every sip. Finally, we escaped and moseyed on over to the second event George had going on, a game show based on the popular Match Game of the 70's. Contestants filled in the blanks to match answers with the six celebrity panelists who were frequent guests on George's radio show, Coast to Coast AM, which included Dannion Brinkley—whose Near Death Experience during twenty-eight minutes of clinical death is perhaps the world's most well known—and David Wilcock—professional lecturer, filmmaker and researcher of ancient civilizations. George was the emcee. It was a fun way to end the day, and sitting in the event ensured my credit card would remain in my wallet.

After the game show, we headed over to Wolfgang's Steakhouse to meet George for dinner. Adolfo was performing, so we snagged three seats at the bar near the piano. George, ever the prankster, whispered to me that the guy who was sitting on Julie's left—a dark-haired middle-aged man wearing a baseball cap—just got let out of an insane asylum.

"Whaaa? George, how do you know that?"

"I heard him talking to his doctor on the phone."

"But it's so loud here, how did you hear him?"

"He was at the expo, he followed me here."

"George, come on, you're pulling my leg..."

George remained serious. "He was sitting in the front row."

I looked over at the guy. He was chatting with Julie, and they were laughing. He offered her some of his lobster-mashed potatoes.

I texted Julie, "Be careful, George says the guy next to you is insane."

Julie rolled her eyes at me and kept on flirting, a better judge of George's antics than I am.

I asked the bartender, Bob if he recognized the lunatic.

"Oh, yeah, he's here all the time. Nice guy."

Okay, so George was typically just having some fun teasing us. Julie was safe.

I glanced over at the piano. Adolfo was playing my favorite instrumental tune that he composed, Concerto in G. My guy is so talented. His love and gift of music brought light to Wolfgang's, sharing his creativity and passion with those souls who walked through the doors. I thought back to when we first met on a balmy night in May of 2001 when my friend Sabrina invited me to have dinner at the piano bar in Playa Del Rey where Adolfo was performing. I was newly relocated from Chicago to Los Angeles after the untimely death of my father. I was skinny as a pencil from the stress and grief, sporting a pixie cut, unemployed, and trying to figure out what to do with the next fifty years of my life. Despite his lack of attraction to skinny women with short hair, Adolfo saw my light shine through and immediately broke it off with the woman he was casually dating, explaining he'd met someone special.

Our relationship has been especially *picante*, that is for sure, with power struggles and differences of opinion, but when we finally could relax into letting each other just be, that is when the magic happened, the joy of just being together.

I felt great and grateful, spirit renewed, yet I'll admit I was still filled with trepidation at the upcoming healing sessions for the two sisters, Laurie and Kim.

Their friend Kylie, my client who had galloped happily on into the sunset with her Prince after several crystal healing sessions with me, gifted a session to the sisters. "I want them to experience what I did," she told me. "I especially want them to experience an angel reading. The messages that I got were incredible."

Fortunately, the sessions with Kylie had taken place several months prior to the infiltration of low vibrational energy. I'd resumed my spiritual work after the Expo and hoped I was ready.

It was a drizzly day, so my sanctuary was especially cozy with candles glowing, the scent of freshly burned sage, and lavender oil. Neither sister had ever tried energy healing, so they were eager to experience it. Laurie waited in the living room with a cup of tea and her laptop. Macie played hostess keeping her company while Kim received her healing session. Then they switched places.

I was in my element. It felt amazing to be giving sessions again. The energy was powerful, and in my soul, I knew my future lay in this work.

Then came the angel readings. If I didn't offer them, Kylie would be disappointed, and she was my best client. Linda's spirit guide, Mike the musician, had said that my small board was not good for my spirit, and that I should use my large blue angel board instead. However, the small board was so much easier to work with since the letters were so close together. I debated with myself and decided to use the small board anyway.

I had the ladies wait in the living room while I put my Reiki table away. A cool idea came to me. I moved my small round table that was covered with a beautiful green and black silk scarf into the middle of the room, along with my purple velvet armchair, then placed my little board on it surrounded by a few powerful crystals, and statuettes of Jesus, Mary, and St. Charbel. I said a prayer of protection and asked the angels to please be accurate in the reading. I was also a little worried because of the time I'd tried to give Adolfo a session and nothing happened. And an incident a few months prior came to mind when a client wanted a reading at the end of her healing session, and my angel Thomas answered me on the board and apologized but said, "Everyone is in a meeting right now." How embarrassing. I want to add that I knew zero about these women, not their professions, whether they were single or married, where they lived, or even their last names. Maybe that was a plus, however, because whatever came through couldn't be coming from my subconscious.

I invited the ladies into the room and had them sit on the love seat. The setup was inviting, magical even. I explained how I work, that I channel the angels through the board and whatever a client needed to know right then is what would most likely come through.

I took a moment to center myself and a few deep breaths, and the planchette started to move.

> *Hello, xoxo angel kisses to you. I am happy you are here. There are many angels around you always. I want to give a message to Laurie. Angels love you. Be patient. Things are slow with work right now, but soon things will fall into place with your new projects. Does that make sense?*

I looked up, bracing myself for Laurie to say something like, *Heck no, I don't know what you are talking about.*

But her eyes were wide. "Yes, oh my gosh, I totally have goose bumps right now. Work is slow, and I have some other exciting projects that I am working on now!"

I continued on the board, and another entity I hadn't connected with before began communicating.

> *Hello, this is John. There are many angels here. We love you. Kim, please be vigilant in thinking positive. Because work is slow, you get nervous easily. All is well, and your projects will take off soon. Be clear in your mind, and everything will be okay.*

I looked up at Kim. "Is your work slow too? Do you get nervous?"

"Yes, Laurie and I work together. And I am the one that gets nervous when there is not a lot of business. And I am blown away right now because our grandfather's name is John, and we always feel he is watching over us.

I went back to the board.

> *We are so happy to be here with you. With that, I bid you a goodnight. We angels have been transmitting from the seventh dimension. Toodle-loo.*

The reading was short and sweet. Kim and Laurie were pleased, and I felt good about it. I especially loved being back on my little board. So, I came to the conclusion that going with my feelings would guide me in the direction that

I need to go. I knew the angels were real, and that their messages where genuine.

As a unique Christmas gift I had decided to give my aunt and two cousins a card with a message from the angels, along with a beautifully dressed candle and angel bell.

All three messages were amazing, and re-reading them, I could not accept the notion that the psychic Elizabeth had suggested that dark forces were trying to get my trust so they could take me over. Here are some of the beautiful messages the angels had for them.

> *Jodi, angel kisses to you. Many angels follow you and guide you. Be a good listener, because they are trying to speak to you. And angels whisper in your ear with an angelic breath of love and guidance. Answer your angels in the dark of night for they will hear you so softly as you pray. Jodi, you are a tender soul, and you try to be so strong for everyone, but if you don't slow down and rest your beautiful little head, you will be too stressed to make clear decisions. Be aware that I am here with your angel, Andrew. Angel Andrew is your angel that guides your happy thoughts towards the angelic realm. And all angels are conspiring with the heavens in your favor. This message is sent with love from the seventh dimension. All your dreams are manifesting very soon, so get ready to rock and roll! Angel kisses and hugs, Murth.*

Part of the message to my aunt:

Cheryl, I want you to know how much you are loved. There are no words to express this sentiment in your language. But we angels try our best. Angels are working and are on the job night and day with your best interest at heart. The light that shines from your beautiful soul could light all the lamps on earth. Soon you will be led in a new direction if you listen. Be aware of our beautiful voices and all will be revealed to you and answers to your questions will be answered in due time. Many angel kisses to you, dear Marla's aunt Cheryl.

Part of the message to my other cousin:

Murth here. Angel kisses to Wendy. Angelic forces are behind you in all your many projects. Please know that you have one badass angel here, and I am angel to Marla, but I can tell you one thing. Peace will come to you once you let yourself be guided fully by the angels and guides. The world needs your many skills so please listen to us, and you can bring these talents to light and life. You are a beautiful soul. Be that light. Angels are supporting you. Night time is a great time to think and meditate on your next step. Angel hugs and kisses. Murth, xoxo

I asked Murth to provide a message for the ending of the book. Here is what she wrote:

Angel kisses to all of the readers. I am so happy to be included in this book. Be vigilant with your angels, connecting with them as they are here for you. Angels love you all so much, and we want you to remember this. You are all important to the world. When you pray, pray to God and also ask your angels for assistance. Make sure to spread love and joy wherever you go. Don't worry about problems. Focus on love and light. Angel Murth here, transmitting from the seventh dimension. Angel hugs and kisses, toodle-loo and until next time, I bid you farewell.

My cousins, clients, and friends have all expressed satisfaction and even amazement at the messages that come through, so going forward, I know the path I choose will be full of love, light, and vigilance in keeping myself clear and protected.

The bamboo beating at the beginning of my journey served as an excellent rite of passage into a more spiritual realm, teaching me I could tolerate physical pain if necessary and stay open to something new. I discovered new talents and career possibilities through energy healing and crystals. I've learned the value of a candle infused with clear intention in manifesting a positive outcome. I met my dad on the astral plane and have experienced pure wonderment and delight in connecting with an angel. I was awestruck by a collective of twelve non-physical entities and also their many amazing channelers. I was exorcised of low vibrational beings, and even wrote a poem, perhaps guided by Poe. On this fascinating journey that the Buddha led me through, I have discovered that the path is never ending. I am on it for life, taking one step down the road at a time.

Yep, that's me, just a spiritual seeker occasionally tripping and tumbling into a ditch, but always climbing back up onto the path, dusting myself off and following my bliss and my levity. That porthole I told you about? I'm still holding it open, care to join me?

APPENDIX: DETOXIFYING AND NOURISHING THE MIND AND BODY FOR ENHANCED SPIRITUALITY

"Why should I be unhappy? Every parcel of my being is in full bloom." ~ Rumi

I am so thrilled that you joined me on this journey of self- discovery. My wish for you is that every parcel of *your* being bursts into full bloom. If this is all new to you, starting a spiritual practice can seem daunting. You certainly don't have to attempt everything that I did. I've included some things that you can do to enhance your joy and connection with the universe. Keeping your body, mind and spirit balanced, nourished and energized is the key to a successful spiritual practice and a long and healthy life!

A great place to start is with clearing your physical channel/vessel—your beautiful body. You want to clean the toxins out so that you are vibrating at a higher frequency. Cutting out or down on sugar, soda's (diet and regular) alcohol, animal products, tobacco and caffeine is a great place to start.

Start with some dietary changes

Juices

Adding a green juice daily to your diet will ensure that you're getting some high quality nutrition and nourishment. You'll find a good juicer is essential. Here's my recipe for "Green Gunk." (You may want to start with two sweet red apples instead of the green. Then when you discover the energy lift, try one red and one green, and then to cut down on fructose and blood sugar fluctuations, use two green apples.)

Green and Clean

1 small cucumber

4 stalks of celery

2 green apples, cored and seeded

6 kale leaves

A handful of parsley sprigs

1 peeled lemon

1 inch of ginger root

"Feed" into your juicer for one generous serving. The green and clean is my daily go-to juice, but occasionally I like to mix it up.

Here's a great juice for the root chakra. The Root Chakra is located at the base of the spine or coccyx. This Chakra is related to survival, our body, and identity as an individual. Our health, constitution and security including material wealth are also linked to the root chakra.

Mudalhara (root chakra) Medly

2 Granny Smith apples (cored and seeded)

1 small beet

4 small carrots

1 inch piece of ginger

½ a cucumber

2 stalks of celery

Smoothies

Superfood smoothies are another way to get great health benefits without sacrificing taste. To really make sensational smoothies, it is best to use a high-powered blender. My preference is the Vitamix blender. I know they are pricey, but in my opinion, worth every penny.

Matcha and **Maca** powders – *Matcha* powder is concentrated from green tea, offering a blast of antioxidants, cancer fighters, and fat burners. *Maca* powder is a nutrient-rich superfood in the radish family and usually grown in Peru. It offers health benefits such as higher energy levels, skin clarity, reproductive health, and more. For the maca powder, some nutritionists advise starting with a half-teaspoon serving per person, working up to as much as a tablespoon.

Here are two of my all-time favorite smoothies:

Matcha Miracle

1 banana, frozen
¼ avocado
1 tsp matcha green tea powder
1 1/2 cups almond, cashew or hemp milk
2 large pitted dates
A dash of vanilla extract
A sprinkle of cinnamon

Blend until smooth and serve. Makes one large or two small servings.

Chocolate Dream

1 large banana, frozen
2 large dates
¼ avocado
1 ¼ cups of non-dairy milk of choice
1 tablespoon of raw cacao powder
½ tsp vanilla extract
A teaspoon of maca powder
A dash of cinnamon

Detoxifying

The more your health improves, the more you will want to experience the wholeness of mind-body-spirit. So, you will also need to enhance the detoxification process with specific targets—such as the pineal gland—to enhance your spiritual capacities. The pineal gland can calcify, creating "sand gland." Decalcifying your pineal gland is essential to opening your "third eye," bringing clarity, improving concentration, intuition, decisiveness, insight, and bliss as well as enabling:

- Vivid dreams
- Astral projection
- Enhanced creativity
- The ability to perceive auras, energy flow, non-physical beings, and "vision" with eyes closed
- Clear channels to the spiritual dimensions
- The ability to work with energy

Add these Pineal gland detoxifiers into your diet. You don't have to take all of them. Pick and choose those that appeal to you most. Adding as many as possible will really go a long way with "sand gland." (Also, be sure to switch your toothpaste to a non-flouride variety, which you can find at any health food store.)

- Raw Cacao (add to smoothies or bake with it)
- Garlic
- Raw apple cider vinegar (you can take a shot each morning diluted in water)
- Gogi Berries (great as a snack or to add to smoothies)
- Cilantro (add to salads or cooking)
- Hemp seeds (I like to add hemp seeds to salads or in my baking)
- Noni juice
- Bananas
- Coconut oil (wonderful to cook with or even stir a teaspoon into your tea)
- Seaweed (easy eat wrapped around sushi)
- Chlorella (take in capsule form)
- Spirulina (these can be taken in capsule form)
- Blue-green algae (you can find this at a health food store in capsule form)
- Iodine (I take this in liquid form and only one drop per day)
- Ginseng (take in capsule form)
- Bentonite Clay (mix a spoonful in water and drink)
- Blue skate liver oil (take in capsule form)
- Chlorophyll (take in capsule form)

Meals

Try this amazing vegan soup to nourish you on a cold night. I make a large batch and keep it in the fridge to heat up for a quick lunch or soothing treat in the evening. The carrots make it sweet, the ginger gives it a zing, and the tofu makes it creamy. You'll need a high-powered blender, like a Vita-mix. They can be pricey, but worth every penny. It's an investment in your health and well-being.

Carrot Ginger Tofu Soup

2 cups peeled and chopped carrots

¼ small onion peeled and chopped

4 cloves of garlic, peeled and chopped

2 tablespoons olive oil

1 tablespoon chopped ginger root

2 cups vegetable broth

¼ cup refrigerated tofu

Pinch of pink sea salt

Pinch of black pepper

1. Heat oil in a skillet, add some of the broth. Sauté carrots, onion, and garlic until carrots are tender. Place into the Vitamix. (OR: Let cool and place in a high-powered blender.)
2. Add salt, pepper, ginger, tofu, and vegetable broth into the Vitamix and secure the lid. Select "hot soups" program. Start the machine and allow it to complete the cycle. (OR: After adding the above ingredients, blend and reheat.)

Of course you'll want to get your **greens** in. A nice big, fresh salad will do the trick, but you don't want to pour a sugar and dairy-laden dressing all over your beautiful organic greens. Try this tasty vinaigrette:

Cilantro Lime Vinaigrette

1 cup chopped cilantro

1/2 cup extra-virgin olive oil
1/4 cup fresh lime juice
1/4 cup fresh squeezed orange juice
1/2 teaspoon sea salt
1/2 teaspoon pepper
1 teaspoon minced garlic

Puree cilantro, olive oil, orange juice, lime juice, garlic, salt, and pepper in a blender until smooth.

As a **main dish**, you can't beat Indian food. I could live on the stuff. This simple, yet exotic comfort food will put a smile on your face and warm your tummy!

Aloo Matar

1/4 cup vegetable oil
2 medium onions, finely chopped
1 tablespoon ginger garlic paste
1 bay leaf
4 large potatoes, peeled and chopped
1 cup frozen peas
1/2 cup tomato puree
1 1/2 teaspoons *garam masala*
1 1/2 teaspoons paprika
1 teaspoon salt
2 tablespoons chopped cilantro
(Optional: top with raw or lightly toasted pumpkin seeds for additional protein)

1. Heat the oil in a wok over medium heat. Stir in the onions, ginger garlic paste, and bay leaf. Cook until the onions are tender.
2. Mix in the potatoes and peas. Cover and cook until the potatoes are tender, about 15 minutes.
3. Remove the bay leaf. Stir the tomato puree, paprika, garam masala, and salt into the vegetable mixture. Continue cooking about 10 minutes.
4. Mix in the cilantro and continue cooking about 2 minutes.

Serve hot with naan or plain rice.

Desserts

Life is meant to be fun, and becoming a spiritual adept or going vegan doesn't mean that you can't enjoy some treats. As you know, dessert can almost be a religious experience, especially anything with chocolate in it. And contrary to popular belief, you can have dessert that is guilt free and delicious.

The raw cacao in this treat will help decalcify the pineal gland. I also eat this for breakfast or as a snack. Chia seeds contain large amounts of fiber and omega-3 fatty acids, plenty of high quality protein, and several essential minerals and antioxidants.

Chocolate Chia Seed Pudding

¾ cup coconut, almond or rice milk

2 tablespoons chia seeds

2 tablespoons raw cacao powder

4 Medjool dates, pitted

¼ teaspoon vanilla extract

1. Combine all of the ingredients in a high-speed blender, and blend until very smooth.
2. Pour the pudding into two serving dishes, and place in the fridge to set until thoroughly chilled, at least 30 minutes. I usually wait at least 4 hours. Serve cold and enjoy!

If you don't have a high-speed blender, let the ingredients sit together for 20 to 30 minutes before blending, to allow the chia seeds and dates to soften. They'll blend much easier that way.

I like to add a dollop or two of decadent coconut milk whipped cream on my pudding.

Coconut Milk Whipped Cream

One 15-ounce can full-fat coconut milk
1 tablespoon pure maple syrup
1 teaspoon vanilla or more to taste

You'll need a large bowl and hand beaters.

1. Place the can of coconut milk in the refrigerator and leave it there until well-chilled.
2. Scoop out the firm layer of coconut cream that has solidified at the top of the can. Only use the solid cream, not the water at the bottom of the can.
3. Place this cream in the large bowl. Turn your mixer or hand beaters to high speed, and whip the coconut cream until it becomes fluffy and light.
4. Mix in maple syrup and vanilla.

Seed balls – These little babies pack a punch! Chock full of nutrients and flavor, the cinnamon has anti-inflammatory properties, and the dates are a good source of essential minerals such as calcium, iron, phosphorus, sodium, potassium, magnesium and zinc. I'll bet you can't eat just one.

You will need a food processor for this one.

Super Seed Chocolate Balls

1 cup packed pitted Medjool dates

1/4 cup hulled hemp seed

1/4 cup chia seed

1/4 cup sunflower seed

1/4 cup cocoa powder

1/2 teaspoon pure vanilla extract

1/4 teaspoon cinnamon

1/4 teaspoon sea salt

1/4 cup raw cacao nibs

1. Add dates into processor and process until a chunky paste forms.
2. Add in the hemp, chia, sunflower, cocoa, vanilla, cinnamon, and salt.
3. Process until thoroughly combined.
4. Pulse in the cacao nibs.
5. If the dough is not sticky enough to shape into balls, add a small amount of water and process.
6. Shape dough into small balls and freeze until firm.

Ok... are you ready for this? We vegans can also have FUDGE! You might be thinking, *Are you kidding me? Fudge is a spiritual food?* Heck yeah! The coconut oil helps ward off dementia and just one tablespoon of almond butter contains as much protein as you get from the same quantity of meat. It is also an excellent source of fiber, which helps digestion and nourishes tissues.

Chocolate Walnut Fudge

1/2 cup virgin coconut oil
1/4 cup raw almond butter
1/2 cup raw cacao powder
1/2 cup organic maple syrup
1 tablespoon vanilla extract
Pinch fine grain sea salt
3/4 cup raw walnuts, roughly chopped

1. With electric beaters, mix the coconut oil and almond butter.
2. Sift in the cacao powder and mix until combined.
3. Pour in the maple syrup, vanilla, and salt. Mix until smooth.
4. Stir in the walnuts.
5. Line a square pan with a piece of wax paper. Scoop the mixture into the pan and spread out until even.
6. Freeze uncovered until solid. Slice into squares

Topping it all off

What better way to nurture and nourish your body and soul than with a hot cup of tea? Ginger tea is said to be one of the best methods for fighting the onset of a cold, treating indigestion, dissolving kidney stones, strengthening your immune system, and possibly preventing the development of cancer. Ginger and turmeric roots are similar and may be sliced thinly or chopped, the quantity depending on your taste.

Ginger tea

Organic honey
1/4 teaspoon or so of ginger root
1/4 teaspoon or so of turmeric root
Coconut or almond milk
A cup of water

Boil water, add turmeric and ginger and let it simmer for 10-15 minutes. Next, add the milk and then strain the tea into a cup. Relax and enjoy the serenity.

Meditation and Prayer

So, you're working on cleansing, decalcifying your pineal gland, and nourishing your body with delicious foods, now let's calm the mind and feed the soul. Connecting with your angels is such a magical experience. These two beautiful angel meditations have been so generously shared with us by Marie-Ange Faugérolas from her book, *Angels, The Definitive Guide To Angels From Around The World.* **www.marieangefaugerolas.com**

Meditation of Archangel Raphael and the Gold Star

(Approximately 15 Minutes)

This meditation should be done in a calm room with a salt lamp turned on. Marie-Ange believes it's best to do it on a Wednesday at ten o'clock at night.

Materials:
- A yellowish-orange candle
- A salt lamp

- A stick of lavender incense
- A yellowish-orange rose for healing or for all other requests. A red rose for love.
- A meditation cushion

Meditation:

1. Light the candle and the salt lamp, and burn the incense.
2. Pluck the petals off the rose and place the petals around your meditation cushion.
3. Sit down on your cushion and place your hands on your thighs, with your palms open. Each thumb and index finger should barely be touching. Close your eyes.
4. Invoke angel Raphael. Give him a few minutes to come to you.
5. Visualize a star with golden light shining in front of your eyes. The star shines more and more. It transforms into a golden star. Open your third eye chakra. Feel the expansion of your chakra. Let Raphael's gold star enter into your third eye. Feel the gold star's benefits inundating your head with Raphael's light of love and goodness. Let the star descend into your throat, into your chest, and into your heart.
6. Picture Raphael. He may appear as a huge angel with great big wings extended into the air, or simply as an astonishingly beautiful face. Ask Raphael for what you want.
7. Empty your spirit. Look at Raphael. Allow enough time for the archangel's answer to come.
8. Open your eyes. Thank Raphael.

Take your time before regaining ordinary consciousness.

Prayer of the Golden Ray for Success and Prosperity
(Approximately 3 Minutes)

If you want personal fulfillment or wish to be at the peak of your professional life and experience financial success, recite the prayer of the golden ray. It will bring light and grandeur into your existence. It's best to do this prayer in the morning, at sunrise. Its effectiveness increases by reciting it regularly, each morning for seven weeks.

Materials:
- A gold candle
- Pine incense

Prayer:
1. Light the candle.
2. Burn the incense. Invoke angel Cherubiel, Gabriel, Sandalphon, or an angel of abundance and success:

Holy angel (call him by his name),
Give me abundance, wealth, and power,
Send your golden ray upon my life,
Open the path of success for me,
Give me your benefits,
I pledge to use them with goodness and generosity,
I shall be eternally grateful,
Amen

Before extinguishing the candle and finishing your prayer, cross your arms over your chest and say: *Let it be so.*

I wish you the best on your path. Be gentle with yourself; life is a journey. Keep me posted on your progress. I look forward to hearing from you. Until we meet again!

XOXO

Love,

Marla

About The Author

Born in Tacoma, Washington, "The City of Destiny," Marla was destined to move to Los Angeles where she shoots her arrow of love on a daily basis as a professional matchmaker, helping countless couples connect with their soul mates.

She is the author of two other memoirs, *Diary of a Beverly Hills Matchmaker* and *Hearts on the Line*. Marla has been interviewed on the Today Show, WGN Chicago Morning News, San Diego Living, Urban Rush, CTV Calgary, Better TV, KUSI San Diego Morning Show, and over 100 radio shows including Coast to Coast AM with George Noory.

Her husband Adolfo has asked her, "Marlita, do you want to go to the moon too?" referring to her many interests—a true Gemini. Yet nothing has fascinated her like her profound adventure far beyond the moon and into the vastness of cosmic spirituality.

Visit Marla's website: www.marlamartenson.com.

CPSIA information can be obtained
at www.ICGtesting.com
Printed in the USA
LVOW04s1942130916

504425LV00001B/195/P

9 780997 566406